BELGIAN BEER TRAILS

HOPPY MEDIA

LANNOO

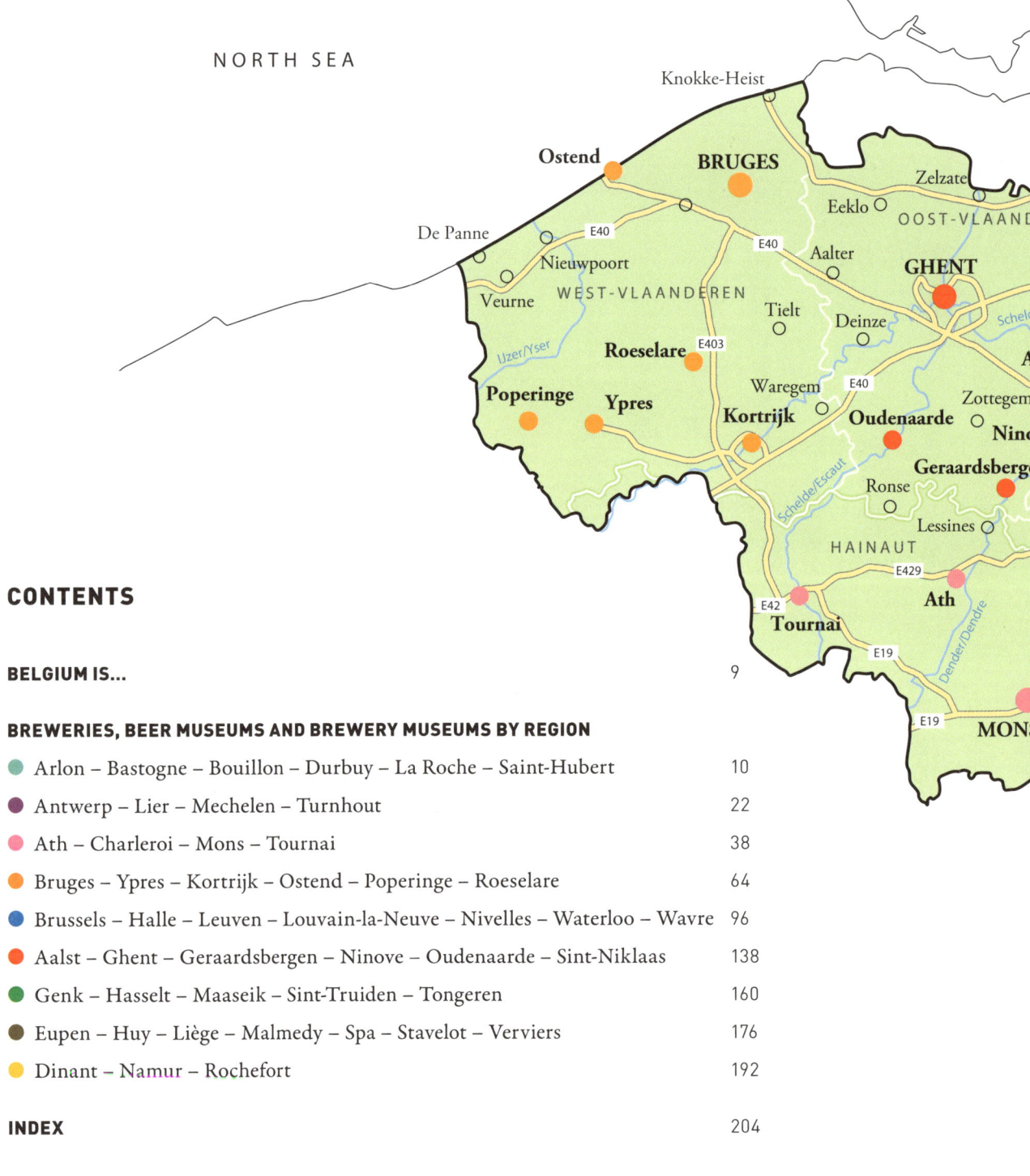

CONTENTS

BELGIUM IS... 9

BREWERIES, BEER MUSEUMS AND BREWERY MUSEUMS BY REGION

- Arlon – Bastogne – Bouillon – Durbuy – La Roche – Saint-Hubert 10
- Antwerp – Lier – Mechelen – Turnhout 22
- Ath – Charleroi – Mons – Tournai 38
- Bruges – Ypres – Kortrijk – Ostend – Poperinge – Roeselare 64
- Brussels – Halle – Leuven – Louvain-la-Neuve – Nivelles – Waterloo – Wavre 96
- Aalst – Ghent – Geraardsbergen – Ninove – Oudenaarde – Sint-Niklaas 138
- Genk – Hasselt – Maaseik – Sint-Truiden – Tongeren 160
- Eupen – Huy – Liège – Malmedy – Spa – Stavelot – Verviers 176
- Dinant – Namur – Rochefort 192

INDEX 204

ACKNOWLEDGEMENT 207

Unfortunately, not all of the links included in this book lead to websites or pages in the English language.
If you have specific questions or wish to make a reservation, please send an email to the contact address listed. In most cases, you will receive a response in English.

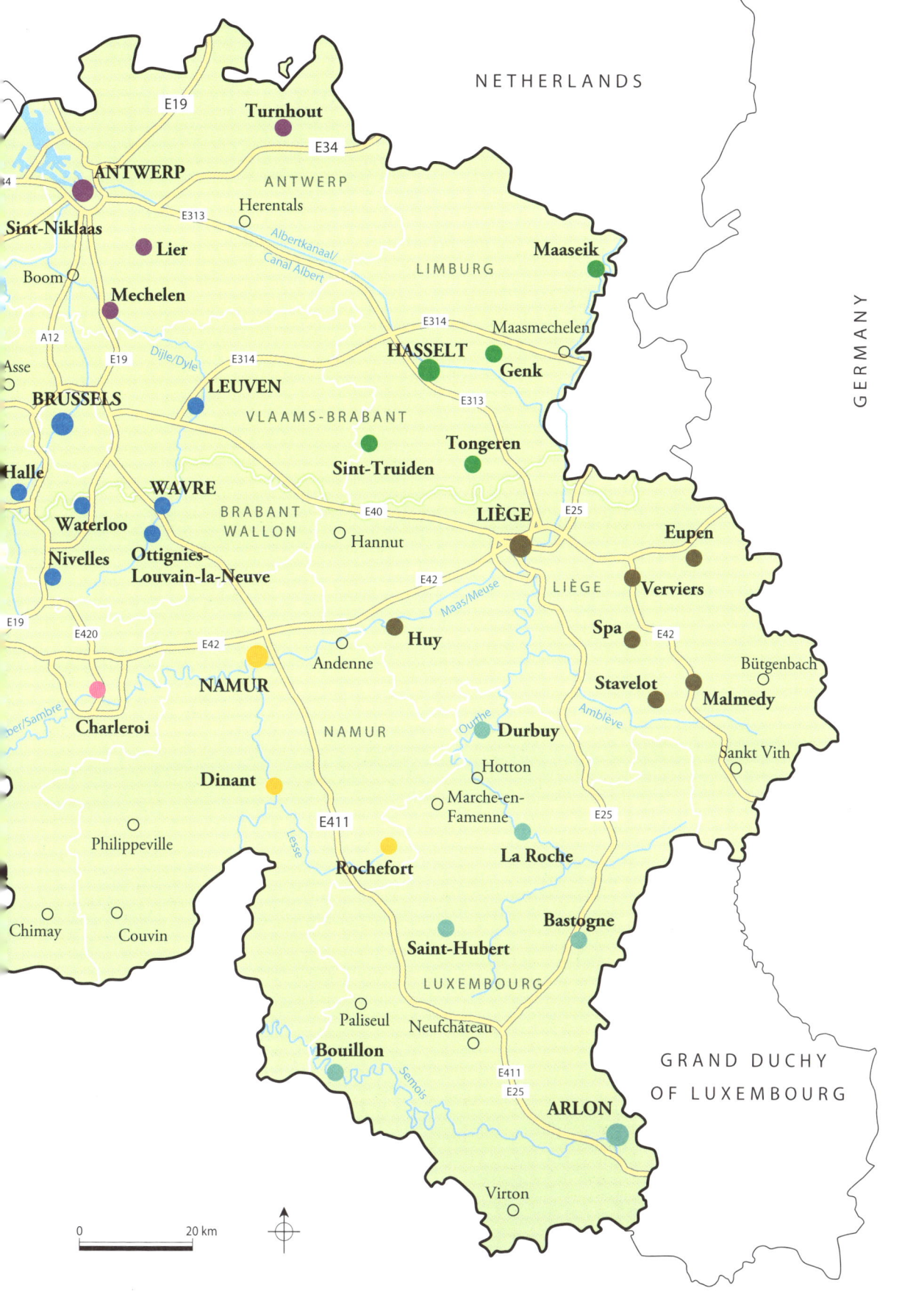

Belgium is...

Admittedly, you may struggle to find us on the global map. Belgium is that small dot on the North Sea just across from Southern England. Yes, you have spotted us! Between the Netherlands, Luxembourg, Germany and France. We may be small but we have a big reputation. Our cities of art and culture: Brussels, Antwerp, Ghent and Bruges are known all over the world. The fiery city of Liège steered a course that was completely its own for a thousand years. Belgium is also the country of cycling legend Eddy Merckx and top tennis players Kim Clijsters and Justine Henin. In Bruges time appears to stand still. Here you can admire the art of medieval painting and architecture. Brussels will surprise you with Magritte's surrealist paintings and its art nouveau architecture designed by Horta. Cartoonist Hergé, the spiritual father of Tintin, is known for his 'clear lines' up to this day. The Dardenne brothers have gained a following through their realistic cinema. Toots Thielemans first introduced the mouth organ to jazz music. The Antwerp Six (Antwerpse Zes) took the international fashion scene by storm. The author Georges Simenon introduced his Chief Inspector Maigret to the world. Belgium is the country of beguinages, belfries, carillons and tapestries. And the town of Spa lent its name to spa resorts far and wide. The North Sea coast is perfect for soaking up the sunshine and blowing the cobwebs away. The south and the east of our country provide a surprising array of green. The forests of the Ardennes never cease to amaze you, whether covered by a white winter carpet, coloured in the fresh green of spring, baking under a leaden summer sun or clad in the most beautiful autumn colours. Belgium is an intriguing small country with plenty to discover. There is no need to travel far as we are not familiar with the concept of distance. Have you ever heard of hanging gardens, tasted an escabeche or climbed a pit heap? Gorged on waffles from Brussels or Liège or enjoyed our beers...?

From the source

We will guide you through our breweries, large and small. Wherever you travel on Belgium's roads, you will come across brewers. Often invisibly, behind abbey walls, in castles, barns, stables, cafés, garages, kitchens or sheds, brewers are making beer in kettles, basins and tanks. In large breweries you will find them in the control room, the 'cockpit' in other words. Entire dynasties are proud of a brewing tradition going back as many as fifteen generations. Starters are cobbling together their own equipment using materials donated by colleagues, milk tanks even, or buy a brewing kit. They are often acquainted with an experienced colleague who is only too happy to lend a helping hand and share his wisdom and experience. The beer lover succumbs to the brewing virus that has lain dormant for a while. At the end of the road, the brewers' fate is in your hands. It is up to you whether or not you approve of their beers. Are you voting for weak, strong, pale, fruity, zesty, spicy, mild, sour, bitter or sweet? For accessible or layered, for a warming beer or a thirstquencher, a degustation beer or a quaffable one? Tasting is the message. You weigh up all the options and make your choice.

Erik Verdonck

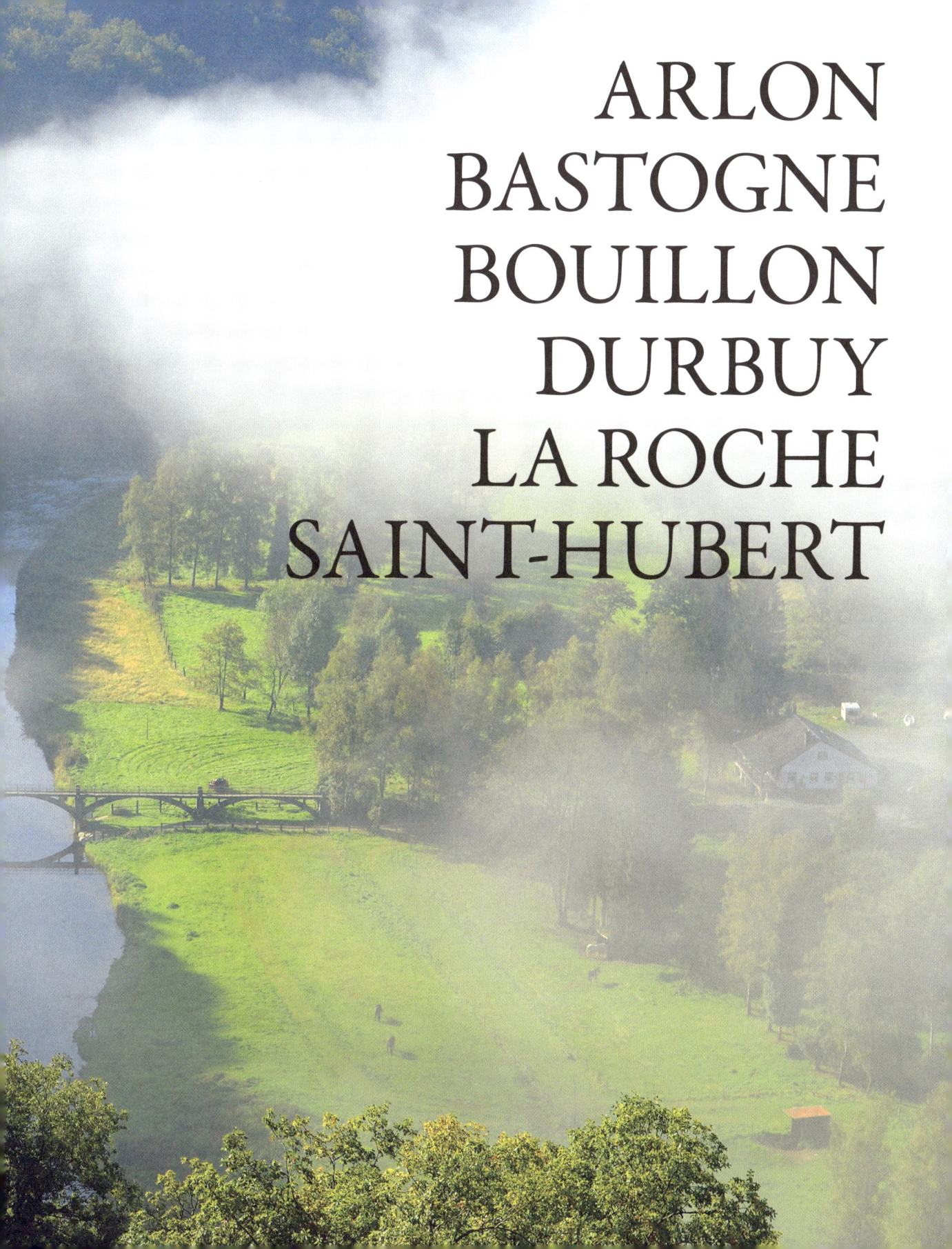

ARLON
BASTOGNE
BOUILLON
DURBUY
LA ROCHE
SAINT-HUBERT

ACHOUFFE (Brasserie d')

Chouffe Soleil, La Chouffe, McChouffe, Houblon Chouffe, N'Ice Chouffe

A stone's throw from (C)houffalize two man-size gnomes point the way to their beer temple. This is where the first 'Chouffe' saw the light in a cow byre in 1982. Brasserie d'Achouffe has formed part of the Duvel Moortgat Group since 2006. It all started with a gnome, bent over by the load of hop and barley he carried on his back. Greedily, he is eyeing up a glass of La Chouffe. This icon is now travelling around the world. La Chouffe flows in abundance when La Grande Choufferie is held in Achouffe, during gastronomic weekends, at the La Chouffe Classic and at the UCI Mountain Bike World Cup in Houffalize.

Nowadays you find yourself in an ultra-modern brewery with an idyllic location amidst an oasis of green. Ideal for a day in the Ardennes, for a weekend or a longer stay. **TIP:** come down in early August to visit the legendary Grande Choufferie.

Put your name down for a guided brewery tour and explore the brewery tavern, the shop and the local cafés and restaurants. Book a guided group tour (with a maximum of 25 visitors per guide). Individual tours – first come, first served – are held at fixed times during the week.

Achouffe 32, Wibrin (Houffalize) – +32(0)61/23 04 44
visitebrasserie@achouffe.be – www.achouffe.be

BASTOGNE (Brasserie de)

Ardenne Saison, Ardenne Spirit Old Ale, Ardenne Stout, Bastogne Pale Ale, Trouffette range

For its Trouffette the brewery found inspiration in the local carnival tradition. The label shows a lad riding a boar with a barrel around its neck: a scoundrel with a hefty dose of local folk hero Uylenspiegel. Bastogne Pale Ale is the Belgian interpretation of an IPA (India Pale Ale). This beer contains spelt, a grain variety typical of the Ardennes. Its bitterness is derived from aromatic hop varieties. The fresh citrusy touches stand out as do the hop aromas which are emphasised by the *dry hopping* (dry hopping: adding hop flowers to the cold storage tank to re-enforce the aromas and taste of the hop). With its Ardenne Stout the brewery brings back to life an originally British beer style that had been relegated to the back row in recent years. **TIP:** taste these beers in L'Aubièregiste (www.laubieregiste.com) in Brussels.

The microbrewery is housed in an annexe to an Ardennes farmhouse. In 2018 it will move to Baillonville (Somme-Leuze). Visit by prior arrangement.

BelleEau 3, Vaux-sur-Sûre – +32(0)475/87 83 66
info@brasseriedebastogne.be
www.brasseriedebastogne.be
From 2018: Zoning Industriel, Baillonville
+32(0)475/87 83 66 – www.brasseriedebastogne.be

LA ROCHE-EN-ARDENNE

Things to see and do
- the fortified castle dating from the Middle Ages
- the potteries
- the Musée de la Bataille des Ardennes
- about the Second World War
- the Valley of the Ourthe

Tip: La Roche is the starting point of the 'Transardennaise' hike towards Bouillon. The walk takes seven days and luggage transfers can be arranged.

Tourisme La Roche-en-Ardenne
Place du Marché 15
B-6980 La Roche-en-Ardenne
+32(0)84/36 77 36
www.la-roche-tourisme.com

BOUILLON (Brasserie de)

Blanche de Bouillon, Bouillonnaise, Cuvée de Bouillon, Médiévale

Brasserie de Bouillon is linked to a beer shop called Le Marché de Nathalie, in the shadow of the Bourg. Jacques Pougin manages his microbrewery on the outskirts of the city. Don't forget to try out the seasonal beers. **TIP:** visit the small city of Bouillon itself, the Bourg and the valley of the Semois.

Guided tour and a meal by arrangement.

Rue de la Girafe 76, Sensenruth (Bouillon)
+32(0)61/46 89 40
info@brasseriedebouillon.be
www.brasseriedebouillon.be
Le Marché de Nathalie, Grand'Rue 22
+32(0)61/46 89 40
info@brasseriedebouillon.be
www.brasseriedebouillon.be

BASTOGNE

Things to see and do
- the Mardasson war memorial
- the Bastogne War Museum about the Second World War
- the Bastogne Ardennes 44 Museum
- the Centre d'Interprétation de la 2ème Guerre Mondiale (Musée Royal de l'Armée)
- the 101st Airborne Museum
- the Eglise St-Pierre (St. Peter's Church)
- the medieval Porte de Trèves
- the Musée en Piconrue for the culture and folklore of the Ardennes

Tourisme Bastogne
Place McAuliffe, 60
B-6600 Bastogne
+32(0)61/26 76 11
www.paysdebastogne.be

Bouillon

BOUILLON

Things to see and do
- the medieval castle
- the Musée Ducal about the history of the city
- the Archéoscope Godefroid de Bouillon about the first crusade

Tip: explore the Semois valley and enjoy the views of this river's many meanders.

Tourisme Bouillon
Quai des Saulx 12
B-6830 Bouillon
+32(0)61/46 52 11
www.bouillon-tourisme.be

DEMANEZ (Brasserie)

B.R. Blonde, Triple & Noël bio

Meet Sébastien Demanez, a former banker and now a firm brewing convert. 'I am not really cut out for numbers; I want to be surrounded by smells, noise, life.' By the way: B.R. stands for 'beer'. **TIP:** taste the beer in Le Coin Gourmand in St-Hubert. Visit by prior arrangement.

Magerotte 7, Sainte-Ode
+32(0)61/21 95 74 – sebastien@demanez.be
www.demanez.be

FANTÔME (Brasserie)

Fantôme, Saison d'Erezée

Dany Prignon may produce a green-coloured beer from time to time. Any challenge that comes his way is faced with courage and determination. How about a *saison* brewed with dandelions? Or a spinach-based beer with green tea aromas? Or one made with chocolate or Provençal herbs…?

Visits by prior arrangement for groups of 15 and over. Beer tasting opportunity. Tavern open at the weekend and during school holidays.

Rue Préal 8, Soy (Erezée)
+32(0)86/47 70 44 – contact@fantome.be
www.fantome.be

GENGOULF (Brasserie)

GenGoulf

A former laboratory worker at Orval is now brewing in the shade of this legendary abbey and produces beers that are less bitter than this iconic Trappist beer but with plenty of character. Friendship is the secret ingredient. **TIP:** visit Orval and taste the beers created by this abbey in the Hostellerie d'Orval, located close by, or in the star-awarded restaurant La Grappe d'Or (www.lagrappedor.com) in Torgny. Visit by prior arrangement.

Rue des Hawys 24,
Villers-devant-Orval (Florenville)
+32(0)61/29 22 39 – contact@gengoulf.be
www.gengoulf.be

↓ Bastogne, Mardasson

INTER-POL

Chili Pol, Hangende Tuinen, Hop & Roses, Plated Pol, Witte Pol, Zwarte Pol

Paul Ghekiere runs the smallest brewery in the country which also happens to be the largest in the village. Taste the beers in the tiny café attached to his La Vieille B&B. **TIP:** Brasserie d'Achouffe is only just around the corner.

Get in touch with Paul to arrange a visit. **TIP:** ask 'Pol' if there is 'something special' on offer.

Mont 33, Mont (Houffalize)
+32(0)61/28 96 39 – www.la-vieilleforge.be

MILLEVERTUS (Brasserie artisanale)

Bella Mère, Blanchette de Gaume, Douce Vertus, Fumette, Mac Vertus, Matildica, Mère Vertus, Papesse, Petite Vertus, Poivrote, Safranaise, Vertus Ose, Zanzi, 421

Former banker Daniel Lessire likes to experiment with saffron, pepper, ginger and smoky malt aromas. 'The art of brewing lies in the dosage', he finds. 'A beer can only be good if you are intrigued by it. What exactly am I tasting here? You order seconds and carry on searching.' If you are after peace and quiet or if you are keen on beers made with herbs and spices, you have come to the right address. **TIP:** visit Orval, Rulles or the Musée Européen de la Bière in Stenay, just across the border from France.

Visits by prior arrangement for groups of 25 and over. Millevertus has a cafeteria and shop.

Chemin de l'Eau Vive 3 (rue du Pont 53), Breuvanne (Tintigny) – +32(0)63/22 34 97
info@millevertus.be – www.millevertus.be

ORVAL (Abbaye d')

Orval

At Orval you experience one thousand years of history and taste the Trappist beer 'from the source'. The well-known emblem, depicting a fish and a ring, is the subject of a legend. In the 12th century, countess Mathilde, recently widowed after the death of her husband Godfrey, nicknamed 'the hunchback', was sitting near a well contemplating her future. In an unguarded moment she lost her wedding ring which dropped into the well. Mathilde prayed fervently to the Holy Virgin and, lo and behold, a trout sprang up from the water and returned her ring to her. The current Orval is an amber-coloured Trappist beer that is slightly bitter and quite dry in character. The wild yeasts provide the typical tart (sour) touch. The beer is only ready to drink when the wild yeasts have finished their work. The bottles are allowed to rest for five weeks to ensure the beer re-ferments in the bottle in the proper way. Beer lovers from the local area will then wait another six months before they crack open their *'vieil Orval'*. Cafés will also serve the young version (less than six months old). **TIP:** order your Orval from an 'Orval ambassador'. You will find them throughout Belgium.

You can only view the brewery on open days but you can visit the ruins of the medieval abbey as well as the brewery museum and the herb garden. Ask for the lighter, 'green' Orval, the monks' refectory beer, in L'Ange Gardien, the abbey café.

Abbaye Notre Dame d'Orval,
Villers-devant-Orval (Florenville)
+32(0)61/31 10 60 – www.orval.be
Auberge A l'Ange Gardien, Villers-devant-Orval
+32(0)61/31 18 86

RULLES (La, Brasserie artisanale)

Rulles Blonde, Brune, Cuvée Meilleurs Voeux, Estivale, Pils, Triple

Grégory Verhelst brews amazingly pure beers bursting with aromatic flavours. Just like they used to, his beers ferment in open yeast basins. This production process results in an explosion of aromas. So, how does Grégory get his beers to taste like this? 'We use spring water with a low mineral salt content. Our main yeast comes from Orval, something we share with most brewers in the area. Finally, we purchase hops with a high aromatic content.' **TIP:** pop into Jean Le Chocolatier in Habay-la-Neuve and taste his chocolate paired with the Rulles beers.

Guided tours by prior arrangement for groups of 10 and over.

Rue Maurice Grévisse 36, Rulles
+32(0)63/41 18 38 – info@larulles.be
www.larulles.be
www.brassigaume.be

ARLON

Things to see and do
- the historic city centre
- the Roman tower and baths
- the museum of archaeology with its Gallo-Roman statues
- Autelbas, Guirsch and Sterpenich castles
- the bicycle museum – Musée du Cycle

Tip: visit the city in May at the time of the annual Maitrank festival; Maitrank is an aperitif based on white wine and woodruff, the herb also known as sweet-scented bedstraw.

Tourisme Arlon
Rue des Faubourgs 2
B-6700 Arlon
+32(0)63/21 94 54
info@arlon-tourisme.be
www.arlon-tourisme.be

SAINT-MONON (Brasserie)

Saint-Monon

Pierre Jacob's village brewery is housed within an ancient Ardennes farmhouse. Pierre serves a hoppy Saint-Monon Ambrée with touches of caramel malt. This beer is based on local spring water; the honey comes from beekeepers in the area and the rest is down to alchemy. The beer is named after the patron saint of the local farmers. **TIP:** visit the nearby Fourneau St-Michel open air museum for an extensive overview of the architecture of the Ardennes. Sample the beers at L'Esta restaurant in Forrières.

Group visits need to be arranged in advance. Tasting room available.

Rue Principale 45, Ambly (Nassogne)
+32(0)84/21 46 32 – info@saintmonon.be
www.saintmonon.be

SAINT-HUBERT

Things to see and do
- the Basilica and the grounds of the former abbey
- the Musée Pierre-Joseph Redouté with watercolours by this 'painter of flowers'
- the Musée des Celtes about the lives of the Celts in Libramont
- Le Fourneau St-Michel open air museum about the architecture of the Ardennes the Mirwart castle grounds and its trout ponds

Tourisme Saint-Hubert
Place du Marché 15
B-6870 Saint-Hubert
+32(0)61/61 30 10
info@saint-hubert-tourisme.be
www.saint-hubert-tourisme.be

SAINTE-HÉLÈNE (Brasserie)

Mistinguett, Lily Blue, Gypsy Rose, Grognarde, Prime, Barley Wine

A village brewery that wears its love of women proudly on its sleeve, or in this case, on its label. Get to know its seasonal beers as well as the barley wine, stout and IPA. **TIP:** a great base for exploring the Gaume region, the 'Provence of Belgium', with Orval and the forests of the Ardennes just around the corner.

Group visits of 5 and over require prior booking.

Rue de la Colline 21, Ethe (Virton)
+32(0)63/43 48 64 – info@sainte-helene.be
www.sainte-helene.be

LUPULUS

Lupulus Blonde, Brune, Hibernatus, Organicus, Hopera

Pierre Gobron established Brasserie d'Achouffe in 1982 in partnership with Chris Bauweraerts, his brother-in-law. When Brasserie d'Achouffe was taken over by Duvel Moortgat, Pierre set up Les 3 Fourquets – in the meanwhile renamed Brasserie Lupulus – together with his sons, Julien and Tim. The 'Lupulus' on the label was designed by cartoonist Jean-Claude Servais and refers to both the wolves who used to roam the dense woodlands of the Ardennes and the scientific name of the hop plant, *Lupulus humulus*. **TIP:** explore the Ardennes forests either on foot or by mountain bike, and don't forget to pack your binoculars.

Visits can be arranged in advance for groups with a minimum of 10 participants.

Courtil 50, Courtil (Gouvy)
+32(0)80/64 38 39, +32(0)497/46 03 21
of +32(0)499/38 21 55
julien@lupulus.be – www.les3fourquets.be

DURBUY

Things to see and do
- Belgium's tiniest city
- the arboretum in the Parc des Topiaires
- the archaeological sites (megaliths) in and around Wéris
- Modave castle
- the Caves of Hotton

Tip: explore the valley of the Ourthe on foot, by bike, on horseback or by canoe or kayak

Tourisme Durbuy
Place aux Foires 25
B-6940 Durbuy
+32(0)86/21 24 28
www.durbuyinfo.be

TOURISME LUXEMBOURG BELGE

Quai de l'Ourthe 9,
B-6980 La Roche-en-Ardenne
+32(0)84/41 10 11
www.ftlb.be

↓ Orval, abdijruïnes

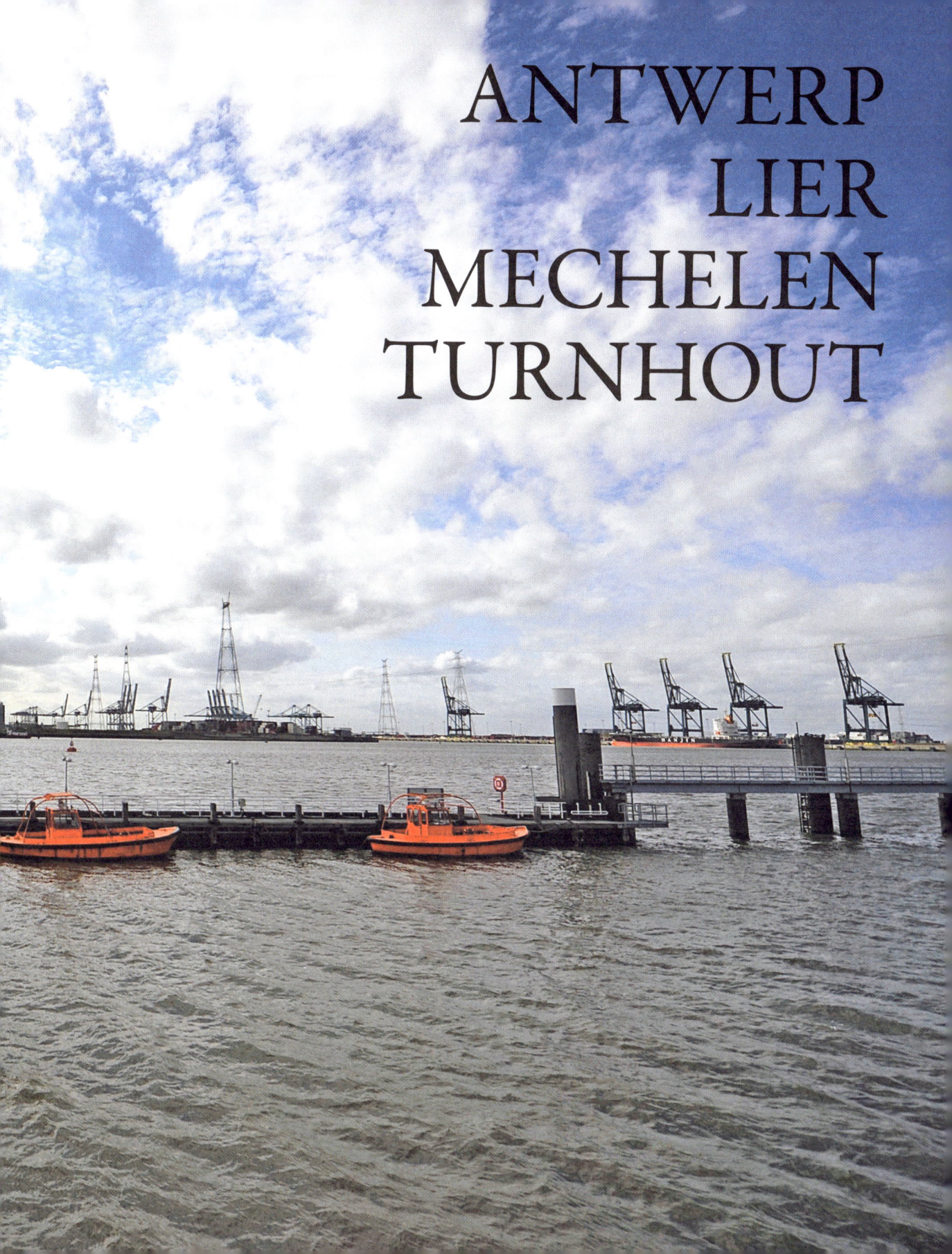

ANTWERP
LIER
MECHELEN
TURNHOUT

ANKER (Het)

Boscoli, Cuvée van de Keizer, Gouden Carolus, Indulgence, Lucifer, Maneblusser

Het Anker is the only Mechelen brewery still in operation. A brief journey back in time. According to the accounts compiled in 1369 by the chapter of Sint-Rombout a certain Jan den Anker duly paid his taxes. This provides us with the oldest reference to this Mechelen-based brewery. In those days the beguinage played an important role in the city. The 'Krankenhuis', the hospice that owned the beguinage, was located in the grounds of the brewery. Several buildings date back to the 15th and 16th century including the ancient refuge of St. Bernard, once attached to Hemiksem abbey but now converted into the owner's private dwelling. Jan's son Mathijs purchased the brewery in 1433. In 1471 Duke Charles the Bold ruled that the beer brewed for the beguines and 'their officers' *'hunne officieren'* in the Krankenhuis would be exempt from excise and taxes. Four hundred years later, in 1873, Het Anker was acquired by Louis Van Breedam and his sister Anna. After expansions and renovations, the brewery was one of the first in Belgium to be equipped with a steam kettle. In 1912 Victor Van Breedam commissioned new malt works. They were constructed in reinforced concrete, a 'first' for Belgium.

The ancient recipes still form the basis of the brewing process. The building oozes tradition from every pore: the interior court with cobblestones, a tympanum in grey stone displaying the year 1625 and the three copper kettles in the brewhall that date back to just after the Second World War. Gouden Carolus succeeds the traditional Mechelse Bruine. Gouden Carolus Classic is brewed with caramel malts, aromatic malt varieties and a quantity of wheat starch. Belgian hop is then added as well as flavourings, orange peel and coriander for example. Also try the Gouden Carolus Indulgence 'limited edition', in which you can detect traces of the house-distilled single malt whisky. **TIP:** the brewery is a great starting point to explore the historic city of Mechelen.

You will visit a historic brewery with its tavern and 22-room hotel. Parties and tastings are held regularly in the officers' hall. Group and individual visits are available. Reservations are mandatory for groups (between 10 and 25 persons). Guided tours take place every Friday, Saturday and Sunday at 11:00. The tavern serves several house beers from the tap and the menu features dishes prepared with beer. Reserve your table at brasserie-hotel@hetanker.be or via +32(0)15/28 71 41. Also visit the house distillery De Molenberg, located at seven kilometres from the brewery, where the Gouden Carolus Single Malt whisky is produced.

Guido Gezellelaan 49, Mechelen
+32(0)15/28 71 47 – info@hetanker.be
www.hetanker.be
De Molenberg, Klaterstraat 1, Blaasveld
+32(0)3/501 82 12 –
www.stokerijdemolenberg.be

MECHELEN

Things to see and do
- the Church of St. Rombout and its spire for great views across the city
- the City Hall and Grote Markt
- Vismarkt square for its bustling cafés
- the Kazerne Dossin museum about the Second World War and the Holocaust
- the Groot Begijnhof (grand beguinage)
- the Dijlepad, a path along the river
- the Speelgoedmuseum (toy museum) for a whiff of nostalgia
- the Beiaardschool
- Koninklijke Manufactuur De Wit for the ancient wall hangings
- the art nouveau winter garden of the Ursulines of Onze-Lieve-Vrouw-Waver

Tip: Planckendael Zoo; in summer, it can be reached by boat from Mechelen

Toerisme Mechelen
Hallestraat 2-4-6
B-2800 Mechelen
+32(0)70/22 00 08
visit@mechelen.be
www.toerisme.mechelen.be

↓ Mechelen, Dijle

ANTWERPSE BROUW COMPAGNIE

Bootjesbier, Seefbier

Until 1976 the steam turbines of the Noorderpershuis (1887) were driving ship lock doors and bridges in the port of Antwerp. This historic building in the old docks area, near the trendy Eilandje, now houses a brand new microbrewery. Use it as a basis to explore the stylish northern parts of the city: Park Spoor Noord, the 'Eilandje', the MAS museum, the Red Star Line Museum and the new Havenhuis. Seefbier draws its inspiration from a beer produced in the Seefhoek neighbourhood before the war. Bootjesbier brings a different part of Antwerp city history back to life: the Red Star Line, on which hundreds of thousands of emigrants sailed to the New World.

Admission to the brewery is free. Sample the beers in the brewhall or in the beer garden.

Noorderpershuis,
Kattendijkdok Oostkaai 1–3, Antwerp
+32(0)475/69 32 35 – www.seef.be

BROUWERSHUIS ('t)

Bossiebier

Microbrewery with café and terrace close to the extensive 'Kalmthoutse heide' nature reserve to the north of Antwerp.
Visits must be arranged in advance.

Noordeind 31, Dorp-Heuvel, Kalmthout
+32(0)497/47 99 94
info@hetbrouwershuis.com
www.hetbrouwershuis.com

DOCHTER VAN DE KORENAAR (De)

*Belle Fleur, Bravoure, Charbon,
Crime Passionel, Embrasse, Extase, Finesse,
Noblesse*

Ronald Mengerink caught the brewing virus when he was only fifteen. 'In those days, I was only familiar with wild hop, baker's yeast and oats,' he laughs. Aged seventeen he brewed his first drinkable beer. When one of his sons was born he created a celebratory beer. Later on he would cobble together his own equipment.
De Dochter van de Korenaar likes to mature its beer on wood. The heavy, dark Embrasse ripens in used peat whisky barrels for three months, giving it smoky touches. 'With these types of beer, the art lies in bottling them at the right moment', Ronald states. The brewer is not confining himself to the Belgian beer landscape; the USA are another source

of inspiration. 'A stout matured on bourbon... delicious!' Beer geeks from around the world have now become familiar with this brewery. The range of niche beers is amazingly varied. There is the inspirational Namur joined by other beers with subtle aromas and tastes. This brewer continues to work his magic with tastes and is exploring the boundaries of and between existing beer styles. **TIP:** visit Hoogstraten with its imposing church and beguinage.

Brewery visits available for groups of 8-25 participants. The small tasting room is open every Saturday between 1300 and 1700.

> Oordeelstraat 3B, Baarle-Hertog
> +32(0)14/69 98 00
> brouwerij@dedochtervandekorenaar.be
> www.dedochtervandekorenaar.be

DORPSBROUWERIJ HUMULUS

Arendonker Bruin, Tripel

The 800th anniversary celebrations of the town of Arendonk prompted the idea of setting up a microbrewery in the village. Ever since 2011 Dirk Vissers has produced a steady flow of Arendonker. Dirk goes for pure malt beers, brewed with hop cones, which re-ferment in the bottle.

Visit by prior arrangement for groups of 8 to 15.

> Pelgrimsplein 19, Arendonk
> +32(0)477/68 64 15
> info@dorpsbrouwerijhumulus.be
> www.dorpsbrouwerijhumulus.be

DUVEL MOORTGAT

Bel Pils, Duvel, Duvel Tripel Hop, Maredsous, Vedett

The giant letters on the side of the brewery depot along the A12 Antwerp–Brussels whisper 'Sssst, hier rijpt den Duvel...' (Hush, the Devil is maturing here...'). This is where, after bottling, the beer spends ten days re-fermenting in warm chambers (24 °C). It will finally stabilise for six weeks in cold cellars (5 °C). Altogether, it takes three months before the freshly brewed Duvel explores the insides of your glass. This strong blonde looks as light as a pils but packs a surprising punch. From time to time, Duvel fans hold the brewer to account. A famous example: 'de Lambiekstoempers', a beer lovers' association from the Pajottenland region, challenged Managing Director Michel Moortgat to the following bet: 'If ten thousand people sign our Facebook petition, you will have to brew Duvel Tripel Hop once again.' This beer was only ever meant to be a one-off. However, the petition was signed many times over. After barely a month, twelve thousand signatures had amassed. The brewery stayed true to its promise. Duvel Tripel Hop was taken back into production and is now part of the standard range. Vedett inherited the characteristics of an export pils produced in the 1940s. Your portrait on the label, the concrete mill on top of a concrete truck magically transformed into a bottle or even a motel... this beer gives you star quality (Vedette in French). **TIP:** sight-see in Antwerp. Mechelen and Brussels are also within easy reach.

A guided brewery tour gives an insight into the history of this brewery and the entire brewing process. The tour starts and finishes in Den Depot visitors' centre. Pre-book a standard tour (15 to 70 participants) or a beer tasting (for up to 20 people, guided by a beer sommelier). The Duvel Depot opens its doors every Friday between 1400 and 2100. Duvel is available from the tap.

> Breendonkdorp 58, Breendonk-Puurs
> +32(0)3/886 71 21 – www.duvel.be

HOFBROUWERIJKE ('t)

Anarkriek, Blondelle, Bosprotter, Hofblues, Hofelf, Hofpint, Hoftrol, Hof Weissen Widow

Would you like to be a brewer for a day? Jef Goetele is right beside you to make your dream come true. What about the beers? The labels hold a promise of jesters, trolls and dragons. But before you succumb to the 'hof' blues... have no fear, these beers really do exist. **TIP:** on a Sunday morning, wander around the flea market held in Heist-op-den-Berg.

Visit by prior arrangement.

> Hoogstraat 151, Beerzel
> +32(0)15/75 77 07
> info@thofbrouwerijke.be
> www.thofbrouwerijke.be

HOPPERD (Den)

Cannabier, Kameleon range

Every Sunday you are welcome in the tasting room, a small café located at the 'Laak- en Netepad' cycling trail, or on the terrace of this craft brewery. Taste one of their organic beers or visit the brewery. **TIP:** Den Hopperd makes a great starting point for a hike or bike trip through the heavily forested Kempen area.

The small brewery café is open every Sunday from 1300 to 1800. Groups of 15 participants and over are advised to book in advance.

> Netestraat 67, Westmeerbeek (Hulshout)
> +32(0)16/68 09 78 or +32(0)495/25 82 23
> denhopperd@telenet.be

LIER

Things to see and do
- the City Hall and Grote Markt
- the Church of St. Gummarus
- the beguinage
- the belfry
- the municipal Wuyts-Van Campen & Baron Caroly Museum for fine arts
- the Zimmer tower with its unique clock
- the Abarth Works Museum with a private collection of vintage rally cars
- Spui square and the city fortifications
- Pallieterpad, a signposted nature walk through Lier polder

Tip: walk, cycle, skateboard or use your inline skates to follow the River Nete towards Nijlen and Kesselse Hei and enjoy a good glass in Café De Beemden (www.tavernedebeemden.be).

Toerisme Lier
Grote Markt 58, B-2500 Lier
+32(0)3/800 05 55
www.visitlier.be

KONINCK (De)

De Koninck, Triple d'Anvers, Wild Jo, test brews

'Halt!' commands the white hand displayed on the red entry gate. Wort has been fermenting here since 1833. On the 'border' between Antwerp and Berchem you will find the oldest brewery 'van 't stad' (in town). The white hand is a reference to the white pole that used to mark the border. Here, the beer colours amber in the glass, tastes refreshingly zesty with a slightly bitter mouth feel and an unexpectedly mild aroma. When 'Antwerpenaars', the inhabitants of this city, order a 'bolleke', they really mean a 'koninckske'. The name of 'bolleke' is derived from the traditional bulbous glass in which the beer was served. For many years, the only beer produced by this brewery was the eponymous De Koninck. The Triple d'Anvers and Wild Jo – a slightly sour beer made with wild yeasts – have now been added to the range. Take part in the new interactive brewery tour and enjoy a complete immersion in the world of this city brewery. Find out everything you want to know about Antwerp, Belgian beers in general and the brewing process. Don't expect a classic brewery visit. Instead, prepare yourself for a total experience with plenty of interaction and audio-visual effects. **TIP:** explore Antwerp or combine a brewery visit with the Modeste Beer Festival held on the first weekend in October.

Groups are advised to plan their visit beforehand. The brewery site is also home to a cheesemaker's, a butcher's, a baker's and a chocolaterie with all chocolates crafted on the premises. The house restaurant uses all of these products and serves and uses a wide selection from the Duvel Moortgat range.

Mechelsesteenweg 291, Antwerp
+32(0)3/218 40 48
www.dekoninck.be

TURNHOUT

Things to see and do
- Sint Pieterskerk
- the beguinage
- the National Museum of Playing Cards.
- The Castle of the Dukes of Brabant
- the Taxandriamuseum about life in the Kempen region.

Tip: explore the Vennengebied, a moorland area 10 minutes away from the city centre. Or cycle along the tracks of the old Bels Lijntje railway in the direction of Tilburg.

Toerisme Turnhout
Grote Markt 44, B-2300 Turnhout
+32(0)14/44 33 55
www.toerismeturnhout.be

NEST (Het)

KlevereTien, SchuppenBoer, KoekeDam, HertenHeer, SchuppenAas, Turnhoutse Patriot, Dead Man's Hand

This brand new Turnhout microbrewery is showing its hand in the 'capital of playing cards'. Taste a Royal Flush with HertenHeer, SchuppenAas, KoekeDam, SchuppenBoer and KlevereTien or think outside the box with one of the blended beers. SchuppenBoer, KoekeDam and Schuppen Aas will amaze you with their citrus aromas derived from exotic hop varieties. At Het Nest you will also find beers matured in barrels previously used for wine and whisky. **TIP:** visit Turnhout, its playing card museum and beguinage.

Free admission every Saturday afternoon from 1300 to 1900. Group visits by prior arrangement.

Beyntel 17 (industrial area), Oud-Turnhout
+32(0)491/50 73 80
www.brouwerijhetnest.be

PAKHUIS ('t)

Antwerps Blond, Antwerps Bruin, Nen Bangelijke, Den Zwarte Sinjoor, Het Stalen Ros

It is hard to imagine that in days gone past, ships used to unload here and take on cargo. The water has disappeared but a sea of cobblestones has washed up in its stead. The former warehouses have been transformed into boutiques, galleries or... a brewery. If your ship is stranded here, you will be served a house beer. The mashing kettle and the filtering basin take pride of place at the centre of this café brewery. Observe the brewing process from behind a glass wall. **TIP:** stroll around the trendy Het Zuid quarter of Antwerp.

Guided tours by appointment for groups of 15 and over. Taste the beers in the brewery tavern.

Vlaamse Kaai 76, Antwerp
+32(0)3/238 12 40 – info@pakhuis.info
www.huisbrouwerijpakhuis.be

ANTWERP

Things to see and do
- Grote Markt, the City Hall and the Cathedral
- the Rubenshuis (Rubens's house) with the studio of this Baroque painter
- the Plantin-Moretus Museum and the original printing works dating back to the Renaissance
- the terraces on the River Scheldt
- the MAS (Museum aan de Stroom)
- the Red Star Line Museum about emigration to the USA
- 'het Eilandje' and the old docks area
- Het Zuid with iFine Arts Museum, the MUHKA (contemporary art) and Photography Museum and the art galleries
- The fashion quarter with the Modemuseum (fashion museum) and the boutiques around Nationalestraat
- the flamboyant railway station, amongst the most beautiful in the world
- the Zoo
- the diamond quarter nearby the railway station
- the antiques shops in Kloosterstraat
- the belle-époque residences at Cogels-Osylei in the vicinity of Antwerp-Berchem railway station
- the Zurenborg quarter (Dageraadplaats)
- view the port on board a Flandria tour boat
- the left bank of the Scheldt for a great view of the 'city on the stream'

Tip: the events held as part of the Zomer van Antwerp fill up the cultural agenda throughout the summer; also make time for the many pop-up bars and restaurants.

Antwerp Toerisme & Congres
Grote Markt 13–15
B-2000 Antwerp
+32(0)3/232 01 03
www.visitAntwerp.be

PIRLOT

Hoppergod, Kempisch Vuur, Jeneverbier, Haverstout

Brouwerij Pirlot fits in with the trend for bitter and hoppy beers. The newly introduced Hoppergod can be tasted here as well as a stout: a niche beer in the Guinness style. Guy Pirlot uses American hops and herbs to produce his Kempisch Vuur 3-Dubbel. This beer is not unlike a scotch: fruity rather than sweet, quite dry with a hint of roast malt. **TIP:** this brewery sits on the cycling node network comprising two routes: Gouverneur Kinsbergen and Conscience. A great base to explore the green Kempen region.

Guy Pirlot converted a characteristic Kempen farm with its wide façade into a microbrewery and distillery. Complete with tavern and terrace. Visit by prior arrangement for groups between 10 and 25.

Heistraat 3, Zandhoven
+32(0)475/42 61 95
info@kempisch-vuur.be
www.kempisch-vuur.be

Antwerp

VAGEBOND

Vageblond, Vagebruin

Three friends got together to set up a craft brewery. Its name refers to the Belgian law governing vagrants: those who wandered the roads without a place to sleep. If you found yourself in the street without an ID card or money to buy a loaf of bread, you were swiftly transported to the open prison – or 'colony' – at either Merksplas or Wortel. The anti-vagrancy law was abolished in 1993 as, after all, poverty is not a crime. Vageblond beer is incorporated into the vagabond menu promoted by the Prison Museum (*Gevangenismuseum*).

Visit by prior arrangement for groups up to 15.

Steenweg op Hoogstraten 52, Merksplas
+32(0)14/63 25 25, +32(0)498/18 63 69 of
+32(0)496/15 80 03
www.brouwerijvagebond.be

Gevangenismuseum, Hoevestraat 31, Merksplas,
+32(0)14/63 36 24
info@gevangenismuseum.be
www.gevangenismuseum.be

SCHELDEBROUWERIJ

Dulle Griet, HopRuiter, Krab, Lamme Goedzak, Oesterstout, Strandgaper, 'n Toeback, Wildebok, Witheer, Zeezuiper

The Scheldebrouwerij produces blond and dark beers as well as a triple and a white beer. This brewer's *Oesterstout* (oyster stout) is filtered through a bed of oyster shells to provide its characteristic, mineral touch. You can tell these beers apart through the two house yeasts and the various hops and malts used. For his HopRuiter the brewer uses *dry hopping*. For an extra dose of hop bitter, hop is added during cold storage. **TIP 1:** taste the beers in a specialty beer café in Hoogstraten. **TIP 2:** right next to the brewery you will find specialty beer shop Bierparadijs (www.bier-paradijs.be).

This brewery is not open to the public.

Wenenstraat 7, Meer – +32(0)3/665 36 96
www.scheldebrouwerij.be

WELDEBROUCK

Heindonker, Weldebrouck Tripel

Luc Piessens always dreamt of having his own brewery and has now turned his dreams into reality. Visit Luc at this microbrewery halfway between Antwerp and Brussels. **TIP:** take the opportunity to visit the nearby Den Triest brewery (in the Brussels-Louvain region); it is easily reached by bike Visit by prior arrangement.

Gezondheidsstraat 37, Willebroek
+32(0)484/40 38 00
info@weldebrouck
www.weldebrouck.be

Mechelen, Grote Markt

WESTMALLE (Abdij)

Westmalle Dubbel en Tripel

Westmalle is an oasis of peace and quiet. Westmalle strives to be an abbey with brewery attached and not the other way around. In the opinion of the sales manager, Guido Bastiaensen, 'Growth often dilutes the range'. 'We want to take the utmost care in producing our beers. Just take the way we administer the hops. If the hop cones are damaged we will not use them.' The raison d'être of this Trappist beer lies in authenticity. It is an honest product without any additives, brewed with varieties of noble hops from Germany and Slovenia and based on the traditional recipe. The abbey was founded in 1794, the fathers have been brewing since 1836 and the beer has been commercially available since 1870. Westmalle Tripel is regarded as 'the mother of all triples'. This beer type was brewed at Westmalle for the first time in 1934 to mark the official opening of the art deco brewery. The Westmalle Tripel is perfectly balanced. Its bitterness is tempered by the sweet malt. The monks have been producing a refectory beer since 1856. The recipe was adjusted in 1926. The now stronger beer forms the basis for the current dark Dubbel. **TIP:** take a walk along the Trappistenpad (Trappist trail, 8km), depart from café De Trappisten.

Neither the abbey nor the brewery are open to the public. You will find plenty to eat and drink, however, in abbey café De Trappisten, straight across the road from the abbey. It also shows a video about life and work in an abbey.

Antwerpsesteenweg 487, Westmalle
+32(0)3/312 05 02
www.trappisten.be

THINGS TO SEE AND DO

OLEN BEER MUSEUM

The old railway station of Onze-Lieve-Vrouw Olen has been transformed into a beer museum. You will find hundreds of beer glasses, cans and bottles, toys and stone mugs. Eddy Bosmans, an avid collector, owns over 100,000 beer labels from around the world. 17,000 are from Belgium. They have all been categorised by brewery, province, municipality and country. Eddy also collects crown corks, advertising panels and enamel signs. Pop into the museum café, aptly named Het Stationneke. Open daily from 1000 to 2200.

Stationstraat 103, Olen
+32(0)14/22 10 50
www.hemelvagevuurhel.be

TOERISME PROVINCIE ANTWERPEN

Koningin Elisabethlei 16
B-2000 Antwerp
+32(0)3/240 63 83
www.tpa.be

← Antwerpen, Grote Markt

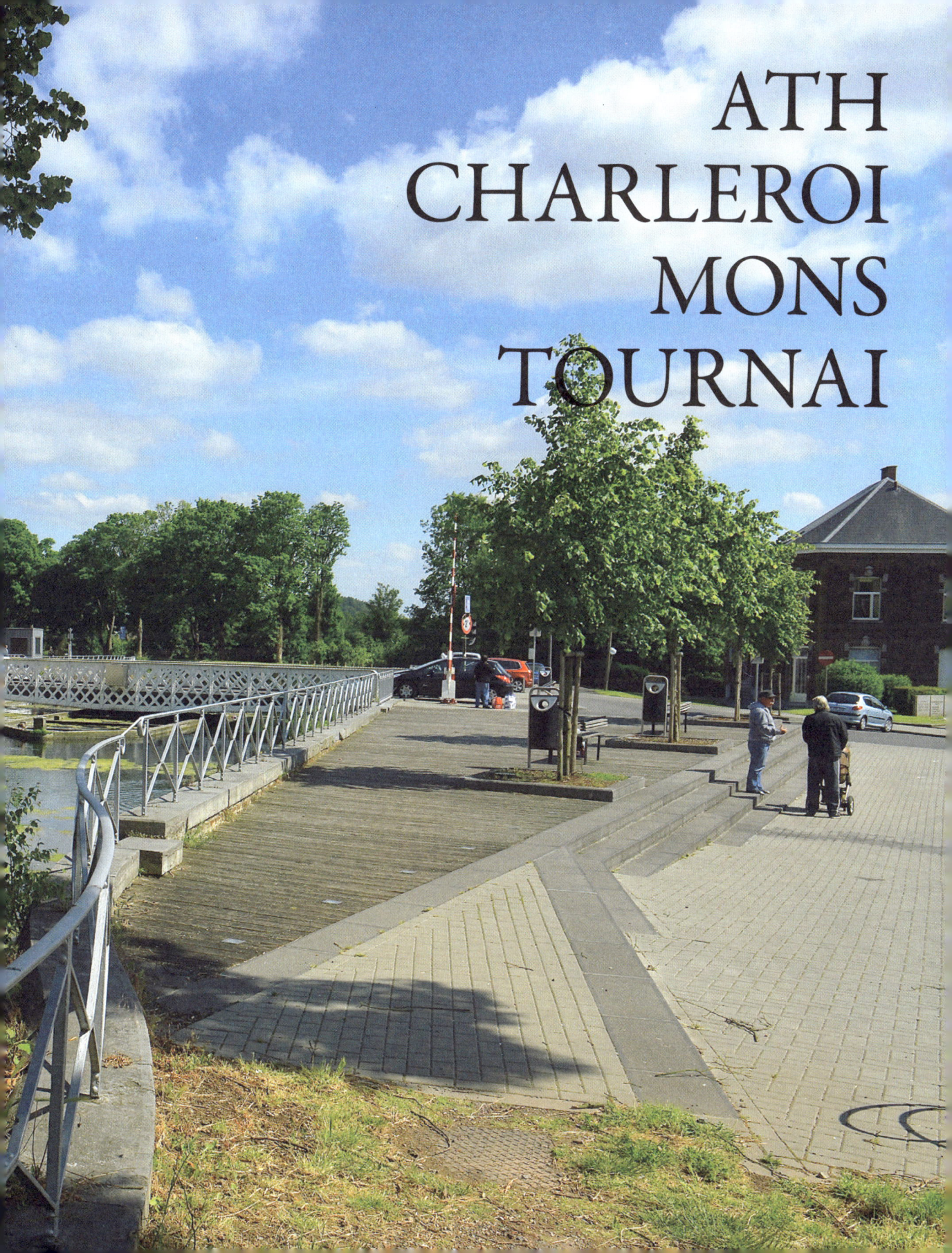

ATH
CHARLEROI
MONS
TOURNAI

ABBAYE D'AULNE (Brasserie d')

Abbaye d'Aulne, Abbaye d'Heylissem, Blanche de Charleroi, Chérie, Jazz Beer

Making our way down towards the river Sambre we soak up the lovely views of the ruins of Aulne abbey. This Premonstratensian abbey was founded in 1129 and plundered, burnt down, razed to the ground and re-built in a variety of styles. All that remains to this day is a gathering of 18th century buildings that used to house the prelates' offices, church, stables, orangery and farm. These grounds were once home to factories, mills, a tannery, a brewery as well as a fishery, but the French revolutionaries put a stop to all this in 1794. Springing up from the ruins, wild flowers unfold their petals. Nature is reclaiming the area. The Val de Sambre brewery made its name with the Abbaye d'Aulne abbey beer (ADA). The brewers use the – slightly softened – water from a local well, house yeast, malt from Beloeil and hops from the Czech Republic and the United Kingdom. Other ingredients comprise orange peel, liquorice and ginger.

TIP: the banks of the Sambre make for a lovely walk or cycle ride.

Since 2000 the 18th century stables have been home to a microbrewery with its own tavern. Pre-book a group visit for up to 50 participants.

Rue Emile Vandervelde 273, Gozée
+32(0)71/56 20 73
contact@valdesambre.be
www.valdesambre.be

ABBAYE DE SAINT-GHISLAIN
(Brasserie de l')

Abbaye de Saint-Ghislain

Jean-Marc Charpentier brews blond, amber-coloured and dark abbey beers and aims for a pure taste for all of them. The logo depicts a winged bear and is a reference to the legend of Saint-Ghislain. King Dagobert I was impressed to see that the

CHARLEROI

Things to see and do
- the town hall in art deco style
- the Basilica
- the art nouveau houses
- industrial archaeology
- the Musée de l'Industrie at the Bois du Cazier former mining site
- the Musée du Verre about the glass industry
- the Musée de la Photographie in a former convent
- Trazegnies Castle
- the Musée des Beaux-Arts for the art of painting and sculpture
- the images of comic strip heroes dotted around the city
- Urban Dream: street art in Marchienne-au-Pont

Tip: cycle along the Sambre from Charleroi towards Abbaye d'Aulne, visit the historic towns of Thuin (hanging gardens, belfry) and Lobbes and the Distillerie de Biercée.

Tourisme Charleroi
Place Charles II, 20
B-6000 Charleroi
+32(0)71/86 14 14
maison.tourisme@charleroi.be
www.paysdecharleroi.be

female bear and her cubs he was pursuing managed to hide in the hermit's chambers at Saint-Ghislain, at the very spot where the abbey would be built. The bear appeared to have wings. **TIP:** all that remains of the abbey are the gardens, located behind the community's cultural centre.

Visits on request.

Rue Delbory 73, Hautrage
+32(0)495/56 53 41
www.abbayedesaintghislain.com

ABBAYE DES ROCS (Brasserie de l')

Abbaye des Rocs, Montagnarde, Blanche des Honnelles

This village brewery bears the name of a former abbey in this region. Brewing started in 1979. Abbaye des Rocs is using underground water, malt, hop flowers and natural herbs (coriander, cumin, orange peel, occasionally ginger). 'We work with pure malt, the taste of the grain. We do not add sugar', brewer Nathalie Eloir assures us. The beers are dry-bitter in taste. Are you after a taste of herbs? Then go for an Abbaye des Rocs Spéciale Noël to taste a beer brewed with well-drawn water rich in calcium, malt, hop flowers and herbs. **TIP:** a perfect base from which to explore this green region bordering France on foot or bike. Brasserie de Blaugies is not far away. Enjoy lunch in house restaurant Le Fourquet.

Whether you come on your own or as part of a group, phone ahead to arrange your visit. The brewery and the restaurant are in separate locations but on the same road. Visit the ancient water mill, the orchard, pond and beehives in the idyllic setting of a nature park.

Chaussée de Brunehault 14, Audregnies
+32(0)65/75 59 99 of +32(0)476/41 91 03
abbaye.des.rocs@skynet.be
www.abbaye-des-rocs.com

ART D'EN BRASSER (L')

Audacieux, Belle de Noël, Belle de Saison, Fougueuse, Gourmande, Lunatique, Naïve

This is a microbrewery as well as an arts centre. Pierre brews in a former village school; Anne focuses on the art. Discover, in this creative hot spot, how to brew beer in recycled milk tanks. The brewer is keen on experimenting. **TIP:** have a look around Soignies.

Visits by prior arrangement only.

Chaussée de Lessines 361, Horrues (Soignies)
+32(0)478/38 73 16
info@lartdenbrasser.be
www.lartdenbrasser.be

AUGRENOISE

Augrenelle, Augrenette, Augrenoise

This microbrewery is part of a social project: people with a disability are involved in the brewing.

Once a month, when brewing is done, the brewery is open to visitors. The schedule is displayed on the website.

Home Saint Alfred,
chaussée de Bruxelles 184, Casteau
+32(0)65/72 82 66
saint-alfred-cateau@acis-group.org
www.augrenoise.com

AUTHENTIQUE BRASSERIE

Authentique-range, Cuvée de la Grande Bruyère, Pils Des 3 Canaux, Saison, Stout

A microbrewery that lives up to its name.

Group visits by prior arrangement.

Rue de Condé 5, Blaton
+32(0)69/58 07 78
www.authentiquebrasserie.be

BIÈRODROME (Le)

A picobrewery with beer shop has opened up in the heart of Tournai (Doornik). Brewing workshops and beer tastings are held here.

Quai du Marché au Poisson 21, Tournai
+32(0)69/22 24 97

BINCHOISE (La)

Bière des Ours, Binchoise, Organic' Brune Bio, Rose des Remparts, XO

The best known carnival city in the country has its own brewery and beer, the blonde Binchoise. The microbrewery is located in a former malt works in the shadow of the city walls. In early 2008 the idea for an exceptional beer was born. The XO, a strong beer matured in Armagnac barrels, manages to confuse the taste buds. With its complex taste of beer and fruit provided by the Armagnac, this beer is like no other. The classic fermentation in horizontal barrels is followed by cold storage and a light dry hopping, using fresh hops, in the waiting tank. The beer continues to mature before re-fermenting in the bottle. **TIP:** visit the brewery at the time of the world-famous Binche carnival. Taste the beers served from the tap in café Aux Inséparables at Binche market square.

Book your visit in advance and receive a warm welcome in the cosy brewery tavern where you can taste the beers and enjoy lunch surrounded by the old malt silos.

Faubourg Saint-Paul 38, Binche
+32(0)64/33 61 86
www.brasserielabinchoise.be
Or via the Binche tourist office:
+32(0)64/33 67 27 – tourisme@binche.be
www.binche.be

BLAUGIES (Brasserie de)

Bière Darbyste, Moneuse, Saison d'Epeautre, Vermontoise

Blaugies is located just shy of the French border in the rural Haut-Pays region. Pierre-Alex Carlier and Marie-Noëlle Pourtois, both teachers, set up a brewery in the village when they stumbled across a beer recipe in a household encyclopaedia. Their son Kevin has since taken over the mashing stick. The story of their La Moneuse endures up to this day. Antoine Joseph Moneuse was a highwayman and a thief who invaded people's homes in search of money. He threatened to burn his victims' feet in the open fire to find out where they had hidden their money.
The light Bière Darbyste is made with fig juice to provide an additional source of fermentable sugars. The beer is named after John Darby, the founder of the fundamentalist Plymouth Brethren, who worked in this region as a preacher in the 19th century. **TIP:** walk or cycle in this green border region, come along to the Dour rock festival or visit the Brasserie de l'Abbaye des Rocs.

Visit this family brewery by prior arrangement. Taste the beers and enjoy a meal if you wish, in the Le Fourquet brewery tavern.

Rue de la Frontière 435, Blaugies (Dour)
+32(0)65/65 03 60 – info@brasseriedeblaugies.com
www.brasseriedeblaugies.com

↓ Bergen, belfry

BRASSERIE À VAPEUR

La Saison de Pipaix, La Vapeur en Folie, Vapeur Cochonne

This brewery is making use of 19th century steam equipment. The brewery first saw the light in 1785 and, in 1984, was re-opened by Jean-Louis Dits and his wife Sittelle. Come to one of the open brewing days to experience a veritable spectacle. The steam machine is fired up and starts to turn over, belts are going back and forth at high speed, and the area is filled with steam. The crushed malt is disgorged into the large, open wooden kettle. The water slowly reaches the right temperature: starting at 46 °C, then up to 55 °C, 62 °C, 68 °C, 74 °C… The mashing equipment turns the malt into a homogenous mash. Meanwhile, the kettle is filling up. The wort cools down after boiling and is pumped across to the fermentation kettle where the temperature sinks slowly, encouraging the yeast to settle at the bottom. Later on, the yeasts will convert the sugars into alcohol and carbon dioxide. Jean-Louis, wearing his brewers' smock, is firing off his instructions. Just like an experienced conductor but bathed in steam. In this orchestra, each element plays a role: the malt varieties, the herbs and spices and the different yeasts. The brewer experiments with his beer just like a chef: with chicory or maple leaves …

TIP: experience a brewing day every last Saturday of the month and then share lunch with the brewer, Jean-Louis Dits. Keep an eye on the diary.

Guided tours: 1100 every Sunday (from April to October) and on request.

Rue du Maréchal 1, Pipaix
+32(0)69/66 20 47 or +32(0)495/25 94 52
bav@euphony.be
www.vapeur.com

BRASSE-TEMPS (Le)

Ambrasse-Temps, Blanche de Ste Waudru, Brasse-Temps, Bush-range, Cuvée des Trolls, Surfine

This café-brewery is housed in a cinema complex on the edge of the city of Mons (Bergen). Five different beers are brewed here. You can only taste them on the spot and from the tap. The menu is varied and features typically Belgian dishes at modest prices. There is another Brasse-Temps in the student city of Louvain-la-Neuve. Both microbreweries are owned by Brasserie Dubuisson, known for its strong Bush beers.

Groups of five and over are welcome to join the brewery tour, by appointment, between 1100 and 1700 Monday to Friday. Pop into the tavern to taste all of the beers from Brasserie Dubuisson as well as the freshly brewed house beers. Food is available, also on the terrace.

Complexe Imagix – Site des Grands Prés, boulevard André Delvaux ½, Mons
+32(0)65/84 94 14 – mons@brassetemps.be
www.brassetemps.be

BRUNEHAUT (Brasserie de)

Brunehaut bio, St Martin

The village of Brunehaut derives its name from the Roman army road that covered the distance between Amiens and Cologne. In the early Middle Ages, the western part of this road was known as the Chaussée Brunehaut. The brewery forms part of an abbey and dates back to 1890. One hundred years later, it moved to a former roof tile works. The brewer pairs respect for tradition with modern technology. Tradition is best interpreted in a literal sense: the recipe for the St. Martin is said to go all the way back to the Crusades. The abbey closed its doors at the time of the French Revolution. The 18th century Abbot's Palace now serves as the City

Hall of Tournai (Doornik).

The blond abbey beer has striking touches of juniper berries, the dark beer features liquorice whereas the Christmas beer stands out through generous helpings of cloves and cinnamon. Damien Delnest, the brewer: 'We are also brewing gluten-free blond and amber beers. The advantage is that you are really tasting the beer. This type of niche beers makes us work in the artisan way. Achieving a consistent quality will remain a challenge. After all, when brewing a stronger beer, the alcohol should not dominate.' The beers from Brunehaut are organic and gluten free. **TIP:** visit Domaine de Graux, a traditional square farm with fruit orchard and cheese dairy, attached to the brewery.

Guided tours Monday to Friday on application.

Rue des Panneries 17, Rongy
+32(0)69/34 64 11 – info@brunehaut.com
www.brunehaut.com

ÇA BRASSE POUR MOI

Rayon de Soleil

Catherine Achen and Antoine Malingret welcome you to their brand new microbrewery with tasting room and beer shop. We meet in the farmhouse formerly owned by Antoine's grandfather. Antoine earned his spurs at several breweries including Rochefort, installed Meura filters at breweries and trained as a zythologist. Catherine, a pharmacist by trade, specialises in gastronomy and food pairing. Together they manage a creative hotspot where new interpretations of existing beer styles are born with plenty of room for experimenting. A real little ray of sunshine. Taste Antoine's Rayon de Soleil, his interpretation of the classic *saison*, his IPA, white beer and barrel aged beer. **TIP:** From time to time, Catherine and Antoine organise workshops with topics including brewing, beer tasting and food pairing.

Saturday is brewing day. You can also visit the beer shop, La Cave à Bières, to make your choice from the eclectic brews on offer.

Rue du Calvaire 21, Boussu
+32(0)476/96 81 85
www.cabrassepourmoi.be

CARRIÈRES (Brasserie des)

Diôle

Julien Slabbinck and François Amorison are childhood friends. They brew with barley grown by local farmers and – partly – with hop cones picked from their own field. You are welcome every Saturday to see the brewers at work in their brewery, a converted sawmill. A Diôle, dialect for 'little devil', is the name of a tool in the shape of a devil's tail that is used for working marble. The Basècles hop festival takes place over the first weekend in September. To mark the occasion Brasserie des Carrières brings out a harvest beer called Basèque

---

TOURNAI (DOORNIK)

Things to see and do
- the Cathedral with its five towers, now a UNESCO heritage site
- the market square and its belfry
- the historic city centre
- the Pont des Trous, a highlight of the art of defensive building in the Middle Ages
- the restored banks of the River Scheldt
- the City Hall with the cellars of the former Abbey of St-Martin
- the Musée des Beaux-Arts, the Museum of Fine Arts, designed by Horta, an eminent architect of the art nouveau style, and its collection of paintings
- the parks and gardens

Tourisme Tournai
Place Paul-Emile Janson 1
B-7500 Tournai
+32(0)69/22 20 45
info@visittournai.be – www.visittournai.be

based on a recipe that changes every year. **TIP:** visit the majestic Beloeil Castle and its domains. Taste the beers in the rustic Taverne Saint-Géry (www.taverne-saint-gery.be) in Aubechies. Free admission on Saturdays.

Rue de Condé (Bas) 62, Basècles (Beloeil)
+32(0)471/78 44 39
brasseriedescarrieres@skynet.be
www.diole.be

CAULIER (Brasserie)

Bon Secours, Paix Dieu Pleine Lune, Blonde de Noël

The Caulier story goes back to 1842. The beers are brewed in an entirely natural way using spring water, pure malt, real hop cones, yeast and exclusively natural aromas. Caulier stands out through its niche beers, the Paix Dieu Pleine Lune for example, named after the former Cistercian abbey and brewery in the vicinity of Huy. This 'full moon beer' testifies to a life of prayer and work on the land, close to the cycles of nature. The brewer carried out a lot of testing and tasting and states that brewing under a full moon results in better fermentation, giving the beer more body and a fuller aftertaste. Paix Dieu Pleine Lune is a blond beer that re-ferments in the bottle.

Discover this family brewery in the heart of the village of Péruwelz. Group visits by prior arrangement. Taste the beers in the brewery tavern.

Brasserie Caulier, rue de Sondeville 134,
Péruwelz +32(0)69/36 26 10
info@brasseriecaulier.com
www.brasseriecaulier.com

Tournai, market square

CAZEAU (Brasserie de)

Hop Harvest, Saison Cazeau, Tournay

A traditional square farm lost amongst the fields. The first brew was produced at this farm in 1753 and brewing continued without interruption until 1969. Laurent Agache re-established Brasserie de Cazeau in 2004. Its flagship beer is the golden-blonde Tournay. Laurent: 'We are making hoppy beers with a pronounced taste, just like we used to do. We are only using natural ingredients and do not pasteurise or filter our beers. We're playing all the registers of malt and hop; just look at our hoppy Hop Harvest.' Laurent often brews seasonal beers and, from time to time, he co-brews with Brasserie de Bastogne and other breweries. **TIP:** visit Tournai (Doornik), one of Belgium's oldest cities.

Tours by prior arrangement for groups of 15 and over.

Rue de Cazeau 67, Templeuve
+32(0)69/35 25 53 of +32(0)472/97 09 53
info@brasseriedecazeau.be
www.brasseriedecazeau.be

CHIMAY (Abbaye de)

Chimay

Chimay is the largest producer of Trappist beers. The Abbey was founded on 5 July 1850, when seventeen monks from Westvleteren started clearing a plot they had been gifted by Prince Joseph de Chimay. The monks' lives are based on Trappist rules that dictate a mixture of prayer, work and rest. The first Chimay beer, a table beer, was brewed in 1862. This was followed by a stout, perhaps inspired by the beer from Westvleteren. The brown La Première was a predecessor of the Chimay Rouge (75cl). In 1948 brother Théodore, in collaboration with Louvain University, managed to isolate and store the Chimay yeast strains. This achievement took two years of research. The Chimay Rouge was followed by the dark Chimay Bleue, originally intented as an Easter beer. The Chimay Blanche, under the new name of Triple, appeared in 1960. Brother Théodore's original recipes are still followed to the letter. The blonde Chimay is best consumed young, within two to three years, to prevent the volatile hop aromas from vanishing. However, a Chimay Bleue can easily be stored five years or longer and will resemble port. Also taste the wood-matured Chimay Bleue Grande Réserve Barrique.

Visitors receive a warm welcome at L'Espace Chimay in de Auberge de Poteaupré, where you can book an overnight stay and enjoy lunch or dinner. Take in the exhibition about the Abbey, its beers and its cheeses. Taste the Trappist beers, paired with Trappist cheese and regional dishes if you wish. **TIP:** visit the small town of Chimay, the castle and Virelles lake, now a nature reserve.

Rue de Poteaupré 5, Bourlers (Chimay)
+32(0)60/21 14 33 – poteaupre@chimay.com
www.chimay.com

DESEVEAUX (Brasserie de)

Avena (organic version available),
Sarazen (organic version also available)

This brewery is located in a converted square farmhouse in the vicinity of Mons (Bergen). Sébastien Deseveaux produces beers that are based on 'forgotten' varieties of grain, oats and buckwheat for example. The brewer prefers to use locally grown produce and ingredients that have not been treated. Sébastien worked as a trainee in the test brewery located at Louvain University and, in a former life, brewed for Domus in the same city. **TIP:** sight-seeing at Mons and a tour of the Borinage.

Visit by prior arrangement.

Rue Hanneton 8, Boussu
+32(0)474/35 00 31
info@brasserie-deseveaux.be
www.brasserie-deseveaux.be

DUBUISSON (Brasserie)

Bush, Cuvée des Trolls, Surfine

The trees across the road only partly obscure the outline of a small, snowy-white castle. This is where Joseph Leroy started brewing for the Count of Ghissegnies. When the Empress Maria Theresa revoked the Count's tax-free status, his brewing activities came to an end. However, Joseph Leroy, an ancestor through the maternal line of current MD and brewer Hugues Dubuisson, just crossed the road and set up his own farm brewery in 1769. Eight generations have passed. 'In our family, the brewing trade is passed from father to son', Hugues Dubuisson tells us. In 1933 his grandfather Alfred Dubuisson created a Belgian amber beer rooted in the English traditions of pale ale, scotch and stout. '*Bush* is merely the English translation of Dubuisson', says Hugues. The Bush beers rate amongst the strongest beers in our country. A quarter of the wort is allowed to evaporate to increase density. Sugar is added towards the

end of the boiling process. The beer is transferred to large bottles and re-ferments so it can develop more intense aromas and a more fully rounded taste. The Bush story kicks off with the Bush Ambrée in 1933, followed by a blonde, a triple and a Christmas beer. Pêche Mel'Bush blends Bush Ambrée with peach aromas. In 2003 the brewery introduced its Bush Prestige: a Bush Ambrée matured in oak barrels previously used for sherry, whisky or cognac. These barrels are now releasing their tannins into the beer. Bush de Nuits (2007) is Bush de Noël matured in barrels previously used for red burgundy and Bush de Charmes is Bush Blonde matured in Meursault barrels. The brewery stepped up its activities in 2000. Dubuisson launched Cuvée des Trolls, aimed at a younger audience, and set up its Le Brasse-Temps microbrewery in Louvain-la-Neuve, followed by one in Mons three years later. With its Surfine, Dubuisson is following the tradition of the Hainaut *saison*. **TIP:** visit Mons or Tournai (Doornik).

Group tours by prior arrangement from Tuesday to Saturday. Tours for smaller groups and individual visitors are held every Saturday at 1500. Taste the beers and enjoy honest brasserie cuisine in the Troll&Bush brewery tavern.

Chaussée de Mons 28, Pipaix
+32(0)69/67 22 22 – info@br-dubuisson.com
www.br-dubuisson.com

DUPONT (Brasserie)

Bière de Beloeil, Bière de Miel, Biolégère, Bons Voeux, Moinette, Monk's Stout, Redor Pils, Saison Dupont, Triomfbier

Brasserie Dupont forms part of Belgian beer history. Dupont beer has flowed out of the tanks, without interruption, ever since 1844. 'I'd rather brew less but high quality beer than more beer of a lesser quality', finds the owner, Olivier Dedeycker. This brewer is unlikely to be overly affected by the latest trends in beer fashion. His kettle is still heated on an open fire so the wort caramelises, leading to more

complex beers. The calcium-rich water used in brewing is drawn from a well (80 metres underground). Saison Dupont has grown into an international reference in its particular beer style: a light beer with plenty of taste. Olivier's grandfather introduced Monk's Stout and the Moinette, a stronger *saison*. The brewhall shows a surprising blend of the old and the new. From vintage copper brewing kettles retrieved from farm breweries – they look like giant cooking vessels – the beer is pumped into modern tanks. The brewer takes his time and allows his beers to finish their fermentation to the last drop. **TIP:** taste the beers in Taverne de St-Géry (www.taverne-saint-gery.be) in Aubechies, paired with a meal if you wish, or in Café des Etangs in Saint-Denis (Mons), rue de la Filature 12.

Discover how Olivier Dedeycker, the brewer, seamlessly integrates traditional brewing processes with ultra-modern technology. Also, sample the Dupon cheeses. Visit by prior arrangement for groups of between 35 and 50 participants.

Brasserie Dupont, Rue Basse 5, Tourpes (Leuze)
+32(0)69/67 10 66
contact@brasserie-dupont.com
www.brasserie-dupont.com

ERQUELINNES (Brasserie d')

Angelus, Sambresse

They are still around: village breweries where everyone is happy to muck in and lend a hand. If the beer runs out, they simply brew another batch. At this Brasserie, friendship is worth its weight in gold. **TIP:** just across from the brewery you will find an educational hop field.

The brewery is open on Saturdays and during the week by prior request (for a maximum of 50 visitors).

Rue de Maubeuge 197, Erquelinnes
+32(0)479/88 78 35
angelus.br@swing.be
www.bierenaturelle.be

FRASNOISE (La)

Bière d'Amour, Crasse Pinte, Givrée, Rétro, Tijézu

The flag of tradition flies high at this village brewery, managed by Bruno and Charles Delroisse. Bière d'Amour is replete with the fragrance and taste of raspberries, enhanced by a hint of bitter in the finish. Crasse Pinte is well-hopped whereas Tijézu is a jet-black stout with dark roast malt. **TIP:** explore the undulating, green Pays des Collines region on foot or by bike.

Visit by pre-arrangement. Taste the beers in the tavern every Friday between 0900 and 2100.

Rue Basse 5, Frasnes
+32(0)495/42 60 38
lafrasnoise@hotmail.com
www.brasserie-frasnoise.be

HOPPY (Brasserie)

Imperial, Redskin

This microbrewery is proud to present a strong blonde Imperial IPA (India Pale Ale) as well as its own interpretation of a *saison*, the malty Redskin. The little hop devils on the label of the Imperial serve as a warning best heeded.

Visit by prior arrangement.

> Rue Caulier 12A, Neufvilles
> +32(0)473/2157 29
> info@brasseriehoppy.be
> www.brasseriehoppy.be

ATH

Things to see and do
- Grote Markt and the City Hall
- the medieval Burbant tower
- the Maison des Géants: the House of the Giants
- the Espace Gallo-Romain to find out about Gallo-Roman culture
- the Musée de la Pierre de Maffle about the local quarries
- the windmills of Moulin de Moulbaix and Blanc Moulin d'Ostiches
- Pairi Daiza animal park and its own on-site brewery

Tip: come down in the last weekend in August to experience the popular Ducasse festival with its parade of Giants.

Tourisme Ath
Rue de Pintamont 18
B-7800 Ath
+32(0)68/26 51 70
office.de.tourisme@ath.be
www.ath.be

JEAN TOUT SEUL (Brasserie)

La Trompeuse

Marielle Coenjaerts established her microbrewery at her grandmother's farm. Wind down in its extensive gardens and admire the horses. Marielle's partner Xavier Parmentier is a sculptor and an installation artist as well as a painter. Jean Tout Seul – 'lonely John' – was the nickname of an irritable, people-shy eccentric who used to live at the farm. **TIP:** visit the medieval hospital of Notre-Dame de la Rose in Lessines.

Phone ahead to arrange your visit.

> Rue d'Horlebaix 57, Lessines (Bois de Lessines)
> +32(0)68/64 63 45

LÉGENDES (Brasserie des Géants)

Ambiorix, Ducasse, Goliath, Gouyasse, Saison Voisin, Rondeau des Géants

The City Ath is home to giants who come out on parade during the annual procession. Goliath – 'Gouyasse' in local dialect – heads up the march. Nearby the Irchonwelz Fort dates back to the 12th century. Pierre Delcoigne and Vinciane Wergifosse run a village brewery. Their Brasserie des Géants only uses natural ingredients such as hops from Poperinge. The beers re-ferment without the need to add more sugar. This brewery still uses a remarkable array of vintage equipment including a wood-clad, cast-iron mashing kettle from 1890 and a tall copper boiling kettle dating back to 1930. Brasserie des Géants has merged with Brasserie Ellezelloise to form Brasserie des Légendes. In other words: giants and witches come together in the glass. **TIP:** the small city of Ath is well worth a visit.

Guided group tours from Monday to Friday.

Rue du Castel 19, Irchonwelz (Ath)
+32(0)68/28 79 36 of +32(0)499/03 96 28
info@brasseriedeslegendes.be
www.brasseriedeslegendes.be

LÉGENDES (Brasserie Ellezelloise)

Quintine, Hercule

In 1985 Philippe Gérard, a brewer, acquired a farmhouse in Ellezelles and opened a brewery eight years later. The year 2006 saw the merger of Brasserie Ellezelloise with Ath-based Brasserie des Géants. And so Brasserie des Légendes was born... What do these two have in common? A passion for folklore. The brewery is located within the nature reserve of the Pays des Collines. The artisan tradition is amply borne out by the copper basin used for mashing and stirring, the wort filtration basin and the hop kettle. Only natural ingredients find their way into the

beer. Quintine matures in the barrel and comes in a flip-top bottle. This beer is named after a witch who was burnt at the stake in 1610. What about the Hercule Poirot stout? Ellezelles is the reputed birthplace of this famous character from Agatha Christie's detective novels. Most beers are decently hopped and taste full in the mouth. **TIP:** experience the rural Pays des Collines.

Group tours (20 and over) available by prior arrangement.

Rue Guinaumont 75, Ellezelles –
+32(0)68/54 31 60 – info@brasseriedeslegendes.be
www.brasseriedeslegendes.be

PAIRI DAIZA

Cambron

Brewing beer right at the centre of an animal park? Find living proof at Pairi Daiza, a world of experience home to animals from all corners of the globe. The Domaine de Cambron encompasses the ruins of a Benedictine abbey, where brewing was done with local spring water. In modern days, the blonde and brown Cambron abbey beers flow out of the tanks of the brand new microbrewery located within the park.

Domaine de Cambron (Brugelette)
+32(0)68/45 54 05 – www.pairidaiza.eu

RANKE (De)

Cuvée De Ranke, Guldenberg, Hop Harvest, Kriek De Ranke, Noir de Dottignies, XX Bitter, XXX Bitter

De Ranke makes a case for bitter beers 'with the real taste of beer'. This brewer uses freshly harvested hop cones for his unfiltered and unpasteurised beers. 'We don't add anything!' For a long time, Guldenberg was the brewery's first and only beer, named after a former abbey in Wevelgem. The beers from De Ranke are robust, aroma-rich and very hoppy. The Rodenbach yeast lends them an 'Orvallian' character. Cuvée De Ranke brings together three different beer styles: old brown from Oudenaarde, Flemish red-brown and lambic. The beer matures in used wooden barrels and wine foeders that do not exude tannins. This brewery's XX Bitter, launched in 1996, was the bitterest beer around in Belgium at the time. Another beer in the range is the *green hopped* Hop Harvest brewed with fresh hop cones in preference to dried hop flowers. The entire malt alphabet unfolds itself in front of your eyes when you are tasting the Noir de Dottignies: pils malt, pale ale malt, Munich malt, caramel malt, crystal malt, chocolate malt and roasted malt. Just add Challenger and Styrian Golding hops and the result is a beer that derives its taste from chocolate, coffee and chicory. **TIP:** visit Kortrijk (Courtrai) for sight-seeing and the Valley of the River Leie to unwind. Taste the beers of De Ranke in bistro Le Potron-Jaquet in Mouscron (Moeskroen) (www.potron-jaquet.be).

This microbrewery is housed in a former textile factory. To visit and taste the beers in a separate degustation room, make reservations beforehand.

Rue du Petit Tourcoing 1a, Dottignies
+32(0)56/41 82 41
br_deranke@hotmail.com
www.deranke.be

MONS (BERGEN)

Things to see and do
- the central market square and the city hall
- the belfry, also to enjoy views of the city
- the Church of St. Waudru with its Car d'Or (golden carriage)
- the BAM museum for contemporary art
- the Anciens Abattoirs for contemporary art and heritage
- the Mundaneum for an initiation into the life's work of Paul Otlet, a visionary
- the former mining site of Le Grand Hornu and the MAC museum of contemporary art
- the former mining site of Frameries and the PASS science museum

Tip: re-live the fight between St. George and the dragon during the popular festival of the 'Doudou', held annually in June.

Tourisme Mons (Mons)
Grand Place 27
B-7000 Mons
+32(0)65/39 59 39
www.visitmons.be

ST-FEUILLIEN (Brasserie)

Car d'Or, Grisette, Léon 1893, St-Feuillien

The Friart family has been brewing St-Feuillien and other beers since 1873. However, the history of this beer goes far further back in time. In the 7th century, an Irish monk going under the name of Foilan set foot on the continent to preach the gospel. Travelling through the ancient carbon forests, also known as *Silva Carbonaria,* in the year 655 he was tortured and eventually decapitated. His followers erected a shrine at the spot where he met a martyr's death. This site saw the foundation of the Premonstratensian Abbey of St-Feuillien in 1125, where beer was brewed throughout the ages. The Friart family is now continuing the tradition, four generations and counting. Several buildings on this site date back to 1893 and form part of the industrial heritage. The St-Feuillien Tripel took on a second life thanks to the renovated brewhall constructed under the watchful eye of brewmaster Alexis Briol. This triple has a remarkably zesty character. The beer has a strong orangey palate, is hoppy and dry with a hint of juniper in the finish. Wine yeast is used in the production of the complex and zesty St-Feuillien Grand Cru. **TIP 1:** visit Mons or Binche, known for its unique carnival. **TIP 2:** taste the beers in the popular Chez Louise café in Frameries, rue des Alliés 43, close to the PASS science museum (see Mons).

Visits by appointment daily for groups of 10 and over. Private visits: every Saturday at 1400 without appointment or Sundays at 1030 by prior arrangement.

Rue d'Houdeng 20, Le Roeulx
+32(0)64/31 18 18 of +32(0)498/86 41 82
visite.st-feuillien@gmail.com
www.st-feuillien.com

SAINT-LAZARE (Brasserie)

Saint-Lazare

Brewing activity in Mons was once again started up by an association. In addition to 'commissioned' beers and their own interpretations of the classics, there is the Saint-Lazare Estivale. Soon to be launched: *saisons* and other creations based on different yeasts. Jean-Philippe Mottoul, a biologist, is brewer-in-charge.

Visit by prior arrangement.

Rue Henri Dunant, 170, Mons
+32(0)495/22 29 11
jp.mottoul@brasserie-saint-lazare-be
www.saint-lazare.be

SCASSÈNES (Brasserie)

1830

The former Brasserie d'Ecaussinnes is enjoying a revival under the name of Scassènes. The 1830 beers are a proud reference to the founding of the country of Belgium and the values that lie at the basis of this Kingdom.

Phone ahead to visit this microbrewery that is located in a fully restored farmhouse.

Rue de Restaumont 118, Ecaussinnes d'Enghien
+32(0)474/82 35 29 – info@brasseriescassenes.be
www.brasseriescassenes.be

SILLY (Brasserie de)

Abbaye de Forest, Blanche de Silly, Divine, Double Enghien, Green Killer, Pink Killer, Saison de Silly, Scotch de Silly, Silly Pils, Silly Rouge, Silly Sour, Super 64

Like many other breweries, Silly started off as a farm. This Brasserie derives its name from the local Sylle River and the village where it decided to set up store. At the time of the First World War, a Scottish battalion was billeted in the village. One soldier in particular developed a taste for beer. He stuck around after the war and inaugurated the brewer into the secrets of scotch. Abbaye de Forest harks back to the former Vorst Abbey and is still brewed based on the original recipe. To get the sense of pepper, you reach out for an Enghien Noël. The well-hopped Green Killer is a Belgian IPA

(India Pale Ale), Silly Sour is a mildly sour *saison* brewed according to the traditional recipe whereas Silly Rouge is a blend of scotch and natural cherry juice. Try out the beers together with a meal at bistro Al Tonnel in the village square. The nearby village of Enghien, which has given its name to the Double Enghien beer, is well worth a visit. In Enghien, Titje enjoys the same status as Manneken Pis does in Brussels. Silly has named its white beer after this little rogue who enjoys a drink or two. **TIP:** the idyllic park of Enghien (Edingen) is well worth a visit.

This village brewery welcomes groups of 15-40 participants by prior arrangement. The tour concludes with a degustation in the tasting room.

Rue Ville Basse 2, Silly
+32(0)68/25 04 81
www.silly-beer.com

WITCHES BREWERY

Free Moon, Texcuus

An innovative microbrewery in a contemporary setting in the heart of the Pays des Collines. It is named after the witches that used to fly around this region. A neighbour painted the witches' silhouettes onto stacked containers. This brewer stands out through its light, dry beers with pronounced aromas of hop.

Place 10, Flobecq
+32(0)68/30 13 01
info@witchesbrewery.be
www.witchesbrewery.be

VISIT HAINAUT
Rue des Clercs 31
B-7000 Mons
+32(0)65/36 04 64
www.visithainaut.be
www.hainaut-terredegouts.be

↓ Bergen, market place

↑ Ath, Ducasse

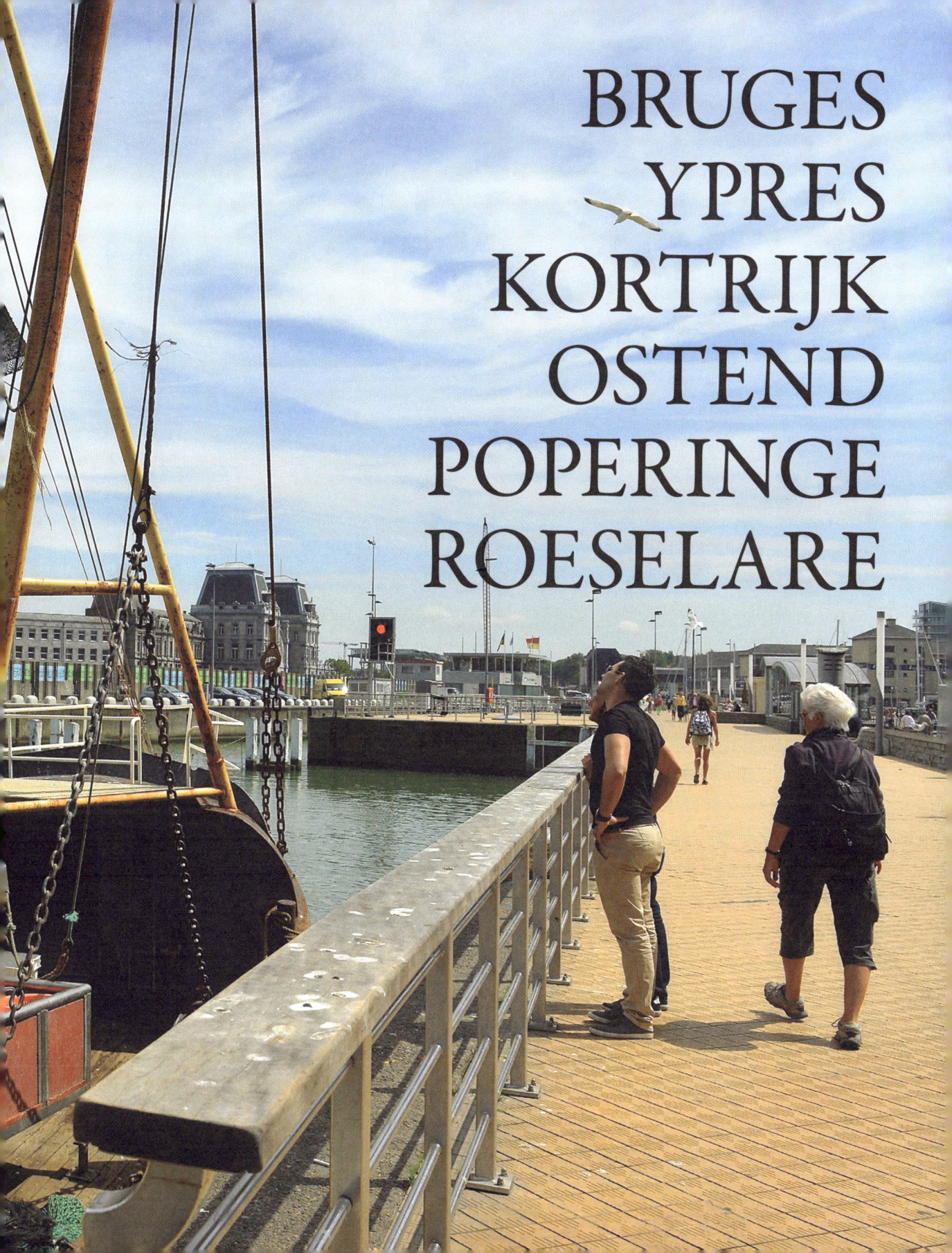
BRUGES
YPRES
KORTRIJK
OSTEND
POPERINGE
ROESELARE

ALVINNE

Base Beers, Chain Reaction, Land van Mortagne, Morpheus, Mano Negra, Omega, Pays d'Erpigny, Phi, Sigma, Undressed Foederbier, Ich bin ein Berliner Ryesse

The Alvinne microbrewery focuses on sour beers, matured in recycled wooden barrels and foeders, but it also produces non-sour, wood-matured beers. It takes around six months to produce an Alvinne beer. 'Most of the time, we use our own Morpheus yeast', brewer Davy Spiessens tells us. 'Morpheus is a culture that combines a beer yeast (*Saccharomyces cerevisiae*) with a lactic acid bacterium (*Lactobacillus*). The yeast was cultivated from yeast strains from the Auvergne region in France. It was a matter of selection, separating the good yeasts from the bad, experimenting with yeasts suitable for heavy beers that would not give any 'off flavours'. Our yeasts are also suitable for traditional, sour beers, a Flemish red-brown or a brown beer from Oudenaarde, for example'. Are they capable of delivering a consistent taste? 'We want you to taste the season, just like you do with a wine', is Davy's response. 'Conditions are different every time and this also goes for the quality of the raw ingredients. Consequently, the taste of the beer will also be different unless you are correcting it by artificial means.' **TIP:** visit the annual Alvinne Craft Beer Festival, staged in March by Bierhalle Deconinck in Vichte.

Visit by prior arrangement for groups of 20 and over.

Vaartstraat 4a, Moen (Zwevegem)
+32(0)496/35 96 19
info@alvinne.be
www.alvinne.be

BIE (De)

De Bie, Hellekapelle, Helleketelbier, Kriekedebie, Riebedebie, Zatte Bie

Follow the brewing process in a restored farmhouse. In addition to a brewery and a tasting room there is also a butcher's that processes and sells the meat of Limousin cows reared at the farm. 'One of these days we're going to taste the beef', Nicolas T'Joen invites us. His beers are named for a reason: the bees – 'bie' in local dialect – have done their work for the beers. Nicolas: 'We produce oven cakes with a creamy, vol-au-vent filling. Cut them open, fill them up, pop them under the grill, two dollops of sauce on the side and a glass of Blonde Bie... Man, man, man.' **TIP:** this farm brewery on the banks of the Leie makes for a great destination for cyclists and walkers.

Arrange visit in advance.

Vijverstraat 47, Wakken (Dentergem)
+32(0)475/23 47 95
info@brouwerijdebie.be
www.brouwerijdebie.be

BELGISCHE ORIGINELE MOUTBAKKERIJ (BOM)

Triporteur From Heaven, Triporteur From Hell

Bert Van Hecke earned his spurs at AB Inbev, New Belgium Brewery (VS), Boon, St. Bernardus and Martens. Bert: 'I decided to bake my own malt to make the taste as authentic as possible. To this end, I had a nut roasting machine converted.' Bert was based in Bree in Limburg but moved into d'Oude Maalderij in Izegem (see further on).

Ardooiestraat 130, Izegem
+32(0)479/68 10 24
bert@bombrewery.com
www.bombrewery.com

BOURGOGNE DES FLANDRES

Bourgogne des Flandres

Bourgogne des Flandres is a blend of oak-matured lambic, brewed by Timmermans in Dilbeek near Brussels, and a young dark top-fermented beer brewed in the heart of Bruges. Visit the interactive exhibition centred on the brewery and its beer and see the brewers at work at the same time. What does the visit involve? In the loft you can smell malt and fresh hops. The beer is brewed in front of your eyes. Through a window you can see the wort fermenting in an open fermentation basin. In the interactive area you learn to – digitally – tap a glass of beer, make selfies to send to friends and family or have them printed on the label of the bottle you will take home with you. Don't forget to feast your eyes on the splendid views, from several parts of the building, of the Venice of the North and the belfry in particular.

It takes around 45 minutes to follow the visitors' trail. Don't forget to taste the beer or enjoy a meal in the brewery restaurant or on the terrace located directly on the Bruges 'reien', or canals. A visit without a guide starts every ten minutes between 10.00 and 17.20. Register at the entrance or reserve your ticket online. There is a lift for wheelchair users.

Kartuizerinnenstraat 8, Bruges
+32(0)50/33 54 26
info@bourgognedesflandres.be
www.bourgognedesflandres.be

BRYGGJA BREWERY

Amuse, Bryggja, Triple B

Microbrewery born out of the passion of four hobby brewers, located in the picturesque town of Damme. Franky Van Brabandt, one of the brewers, trained as an herbalist and this shines through in the Amuse, an aperitif beer with spicy flavours of coriander, galangal and gentian. What else is on offer? A triple, an IPA and a rather hoppy dark beer similar to porter and stout. The name of this brewery comes from the Old Norse b*ryggja* meaning 'jetty' or 'harbour', believed to be the origin of the name of Bruges. **TIP:** visit Damme or Bruges, cycle or walk in the polders.

Get in touch via phone or email to arrange your visit. .

Moerkerkebrug 3, Damme
+32(0)479/22 01 13
www.bryggjabrewery.be

↑ Bruges, belfry

Kortrijk, beguinage

DE BRABANDERE

Bavik, Wittekerke, Ezel, Petrus, Pilaarbijter, Kwaremont

Brouwerij De Brabandere has been owned by the same family since 1894. The fourth generation is now in charge. The brewery is known for its Bavik pils; Kwaremont, the blonde 'course beer' and the Flemish red-brown Petrus beers. Its brewer, Yves Benoit, is lifting the edge of the veil: 'Our starting point is a blonde-amber top fermented beer that matures on oak for two to three years at least. The maturation in our foeders (220 hectolitres) creates a freshly sour taste similar to that of wine. The beer breathes in the barrel. The amount of oxygen present is just about sufficient to support the controlled growth of six micro-organisms on the inside barrel wall. These organisms convert the residual sugars from the main fermentation into organic acids, esters and more alcohol.' Yves stresses the importance of the micro-organisms as they determine the typically sour taste and the aroma. The brewer used to work with smaller, horizontal barrels traditionally used for making wine. Modern foeders are generally larger and can be in a horizontal as well as a vertical position. Petrus Oud Bruin is a blend of a dark, freshly brewed beer with a beer that has matured for at least 27 months in oak barrels. Petrus Aged Pale is an uncut, blond, oak-matured beer. The beer is mainly brewed with pale malt and pale-ale malt which accounts for its light colour. Petrus Aged Pale has an oaky aroma, hints of sherry and fruit (pears), steeped in a wealth of taste with a classically sweet but sour finish and a low carbon dioxide content. It a very dry and sour beer.

Taste the many shades of 'sour' after a visit to the foeder hall and the tasting room. Visit by prior arrangement.

Rijksweg 33, Bavikhove
+32(0)56/71 90 91
www.brouwerijdebrabandere.be

KORTRIJK (COURTRAI)

Things to see and do
- The city hall, the belfry and Grote Markt Sint-Maartenskerk and Onze-Lieve-Vrouwekerk with its Gravenkapel
- the beguinage
- the Broel Towers
- the banks of the Leie
- the Museum Texture about the flax and linen industry
- the signposted city walk
- Buda island, a creative hotspot

Toerisme Kortrijk
Beguinagepark, B-8500 Kortrijk
+32(0)56/27 78 40
www.toerismekortrijk.be

DOLLE BROUWERS (De)

Arabier, Boskeun, Dulle Teve, Oerbier, Stille Nacht, Stout

Familiarise yourself with the work of creative do-it-all Kris Herteleer and discover the meaning of 't Oerisme. This story starts off with a bath tub. De Dolle Brouwers experimented with natural ingredients to brew the 'mother of all beers'. In other words, unfiltered, unpasteurised and without any artificial colourings. In 1980 they acquired the vacant buildings of the Costenoble brewery. Once again, the smell of boiling wort and fresh hop cones wafts through Esen. Creativity abounds in this ancient brewery. The views across the polders are simply delightful. As to the beer? Over to you. **TIP:** see the monuments and cemeteries of the First World War and unwind in De Blankaart nature reserve.

Visit the brewery with its historic brewhall dating back to 1840, the tasting room and the café (only open during weekends). Group visits of 30 and over by prior arrangement. Smaller groups and individual visitors are welcome every Sunday afternoon at 1400.

Roeselarestraat 12b, Esen (Diksmuide)
+32(0)51/50 27 81 of +32(0)498/10 29 35
info@dedollebrouwers.be
www.dedollebrouwers.be

EUTROPIUS

Oscar, Remembrance 14-18, St-Tabernak, Vinkenier

The best-known cinema awards in the world, the First World War, a French-Canadian swear word and a song contest for finches. All of these served as an inspiration for the beers brewed by Wouter Vermeersch and Barbara Pratz. This brewer is keen on using exotic aroma hops and often collaborates with colleagues and bands from abroad, the Canadian death metal band Kataklysm for example. **TIP:** enjoy the beers at Charlou's or 't Duivels Paterke in Kortrijk (Courtrai).

Visit by prior arrangement for groups of 10 and over.

Hogeweg 263, Menen
+32(0)494/39 99 66
info@brouwerij-eutropius.be
www.brouwerij-eutropius.be

FORT LAPIN

Fort Lapin

Pop in to meet Kristof Vandenbussche in his Bruges microbrewery with café attached. Fort Lapin is a reference to an old fort located to the north of Bruges. If you think the name is based on a long-eared rabbit, you are mistaken. There is plenty here to tickle all the taste buds: the triple, quadruple, the amber beer made with hibiscus, the extra hoppy Hop Lapin during the summer or else the zesty Snow Lapin winter beer. **TIP:** visit Bruges or Damme. Fort Lapin also brews the house beer for Café Vlissinghe in Bruges.

Tours available every Saturday between 1400 and 1800 or on request.

Koolkerksesteenweg 32, Bruges
+32(0)495/50 26 70 – www.fortlapin.com

GAVERHOPKE ('t)

Bitter Sweet Symphony, Blondje, Branding Hopke, Bruintje, Den 12, Koerseklakske, Kriek, Spring Tipple, Stasegemse Loper, Zingende Blondine

Gudrun Vandoorne is keen on aromatic beers and occasionally likes to use American aroma hops. Her Koerseklakske pays homage to the Tour of Flanders. Gudrun Vandoorne and Bruno Delrue are a team, managing a family brewery in a historic farmhouse with its own tavern, inviting terrace and play area. The 'little terrors' have nothing to complain about. **TIP:** sightseeing in Kortrijk (Courtrai) or explore the Leie area on foot or by bike.

Guided tours by prior arrangement.

Platanendreef 16, Nieuwenhove (Waregem)
+32(0)497/76 04 12 – info@tgaverhopke.be
www.tgaverhopke.be

GULDEN SPOOR (Het)

Gulden Spoor, Netebuk

Gulden Spoor is the house brewery attached to beer restaurant 't Rusteel. The extensive beer menu includes a large variety of regional beers including thirty that are brewed in-house. The Gulden Spoor brewers have a strong sense of adventure. Extra hoppy, oak-matured... why ever not? What's more, the ingredients for their beers are sourced locally wherever possible. The fame of Beer Restaurant 't Rusteel has spread throughout the region. Here, you can enjoy two house beers, Gulden Spoor and Netebuk but the beer menu also includes a variety of Belgian beer classics. The courtyard affords great views of the impressive brewhall. **TIP:** Sight-seeing in the city of Kortrijk (Courtrai). A bike ride or a walk in the Heulebeek nature reserve right at the centre of the Leie region.
Phone ahead to arrange your visit.

Heulestraat 168, Gullegem
+32(0)497/54 88 80 – info@brouwkot.be
www.brouwkot.be - www.rusteel.be

HALVE MAAN (De)

Brugse Zot, Straffe Hendrik

The archives of the City of Bruges include a register for a brewery called Die Maene, located at Walplein, as early as 1564. This city brewery is now owned by the sixth generation of the Maes-Vanneste family. De Halve Maan has made its name with its very quaffable Brugse Zot, available in two versions: blond and brown. Emperor Maximilian of Austria coined the not-too-complimentary nickname of 'Brugse Zot' for the inhabitants of Bruges, who petitioned him to build a new hospital for the mentally ill. The degustation beers that go by the name of Straffe Hendrik refer to the five generations of brewery owners who were called Henri (Hendrik) Maes. Brugse Zot was launched in 2002 and enjoyed instant popularity. 'People are proud of their beer', Xavier Vanneste assures us. 'Chauvinism plays a strong part, and rightly so. We have fought for permission to continue brewing at this location in the inner city of Bruges, where brewing goes back five hundred years'. The rich brewing tradition of the city of Bruges is documented in the brewery museum.
In 2016 Brouwerij De Halve Maan started using an underground beer pipeline. From the brewery the beer is pumped through the pipes to the logistic centre on the outskirts of the city across a distance of 3.5 kilometres, a world 'first'.
Guided tours are held every day at fixed hours. Enjoy the panoramic views of Bruges from the roof of the brewery. The tavern serves regional dishes that go well with the beer of your choice. Enjoy a beer and/or lunch on the splendid terrace in the interior court.

Walplein 26, Bruges
+32(0)50/33 26 97 – www.halvemaan.be

KAZEMATTEN

The Wipers Times 14, Grotten Santé

Ypres was built as a fortified city. Its former casemates are fortified gun emplacements (in Dutch: Kazematten) and are now home to a contemporary brewery. This brewery's Wipers Times 14 harks back to the First World War when British soldiers produced a wartime newspaper from these vaulted chambers. They pronounced 'Ypres' as 'Wipers' and the rest is history. Another beer flowing out of the Kazematten tanks is Grotten Santé. This is based on Grottenbier, a beer designed by the late Pierre Celis, the spiritual father of Hoegaarden white beer. Kazematten is a project jointly undertaken by the Rodenbach and St. Bernardus breweries. **TIP:** on foot, follow the signposted 'Ieperse Vestingroute' (2.6 km).
Arrange your visit in advance.

Houten Paard 1, Ypres
+32(0)57/38 80 21
info@kazematten.be – www.kazematten.be

↓ Bruges, De Halve Maan

↑ Bruges

BRUGES

Things to see and do
- the Markt and the City Hall
- the belfry, also for its splendid views of the city
- the Bruges Beer Museum
- Burgplein and the Basiliek van het Heilig Bloed (Basilica of the Holy Blood)
- Sint-Janshospitaal
- the 'Gruuthuus'
- the Groeningemuseum for its collection of ancient art (Van Eyck)
- a boat trip along the reien (canals) to view the historic city centre
- the beguinage and Minnewater lake
- the Lace Centre (Kantcentrum)
- Sint-Salvatorskathedraal
- Onze-Lieve-Vrouwekerk
- the historic city centre, a UNESCO world heritage site

Tip: from Bruges, take a short bicycle trip along the Damse Vaart canal to the medieval town of Damme and pay a visit to the Siphon brewery and the restaurant that bears the same name (www.siphonbrewing.be).

Visit Bruges
Markt 1 – B-8000 Bruges
't Zand 34 – B-8000 Bruges
Stationsplein – B-8000 Bruges
+32(0)50/44 46 46
toerisme@Bruges.be
www.Bruges.be/toerisme
www.visitbruges.be

← Bruges, Rozenhoedkaai

LEITE (De)

Bon Homme, Cuvée Jeun'homme, Cuvée Mam'zelle, Cuvée Soeur'Ise, Enfant Terriple, Femme Fatale, Fils à Papa, Ma Mère Spéciale, Merci Maman

In 2008 Luc Vermeersch established the De Leite brewery. His Femme Fatale beer shows that he is fascinated by women. Rik Vermeersch would not go that far; he only designed the label. 'We have several artists in our family and they design all of our labels. So what connects the story of all our labels? Artistic freedom!' Luc says with a laugh. The brewer produces four basic beers and uses them to carry out the occasional experiment. Expect an Enfant Terriple with a touch of sour, a hoppy Cuvée Jeun'Homme and a kriek that has been baptised Cuvée Soeur'Ise.

Visit by prior arrangement for groups of 20 and over.

De Leiteweg 32, Ruddervoorde –
+32(0)50/25 07 96 – luc.vermeersch@deleite.be
www.deleite.be

MAENHOUT

Blinde Mol, Ferre Quadrupel, Hoppa Hontas, Koeketiene

Thijs Maenhout learnt the ins and outs of the brewing trade at Alvinne's. Where does the name Koeketiene come from? Thijs: 'I met my wife Birgitte when we were playing cards. Koeketiene: diamond 10 (top card).
Microbrewery with tasting room. Open every Saturday between 1400 and 1800. Guided tours by pre-arrangement for groups of 10 and over.

Brugsesteenweg 157, Pittem
+32(0)477/75 00 20
info@brouwerijmaenhout.be
www.brouwerijmaenhout.be

OMER VANDER GHINSTE

Blauw, Bellegems Witbier, Bockor, Brasserie Le Fort, Cuvée des Jacobins, Gueuze Jacobins, Rosé Max, Kriek des Jacobins, Kriek Max, Omer. VanderGhinste Roodbruin

The brewery was founded in 1892 by Omer Vander Ghinste. Omer simply named the beer after himself: Omer Vander Ghinste. That's how things were done in those days. Leaded windows were his only means of advertising. This also explains the dynasty of 'Omers'. Each first-born son and heir was graced with this first name, otherwise the windows would have to be replaced after the birth. Far too costly! Five first-born sons have now been baptised Omer. The Vander Ghinste Ouden Tripel is the predecessor of the current VanderGhinste Roodbruin. 'Tripel' was meant as a reference to the three ingredients of the beer (hop, malt and yeast) and not, as is usual, to 'triple the amount of malt used'. The brewery introduced its first pils in 1929. Nowadays, Omer Vander Ghinste is primarily known for its specialty beers such as Kriek Max and Omer. The open cooling basin, or 'koelschip', allows the lambic to ferment spontaneously. Sam Quartier, the brewer: 'After brewing we pump the hot wort (barley malt and wheat extract) from the boiling kettle into the cooling basin (a flat, open copper basin). The wort will spend one night cooling down through contact with the ambient air. It will become "infected" with wild yeasts and bacteria including those of the *Brettanomyces* type, characteristic of lambic.' The lambic is transferred to the foeder hall where it will ferment for at least 18 months in the vertical foeders. Each foeder tells its own story. The brewer keeps a close watch on developments. Sam: 'We cut (blend) the 'ripe' lambic with a young, top-fermented beer we have brewed in the traditional way with wheat malt and barley malt. In our VanderGhinste Oud Bruin the fruity, young beer tones down the sour taste of the lambic. Our Cuvée des Jacobins is an uncut, one hundred percent dark lambic. Compared with the traditional lambic from the Pajottenland area, this West Flanders lambic contains more acetic acid and solvent (ethyl acetate) as it matures in vertical foeders.' Fermentation and maturation provide the typical refreshing, slightly sour taste. Omer Vander Ghinste has also launched the dark Brasserie Le Fort and Le Fort Tripel, named after the former Kortrijk brewery that fell into the lap of the Vander Ghinste family. **TIP:** pop into the De Sportwereld café at the corner. You will recognise it by its splendid Omer Vander Ghinste leaded windows.

Visit by prior arrangement.

>Kwabrugstraat 5, Bellegem
>+32(0)56/23 51 71 – visit@omer.be
>www.omervanderghinste.be

YPRES

Things to see and do
- Town Hall and Grote Markt
- Lakenhalle (the Cloth Hall), the belfry and its carillon
- Sint-Maartenskathedraal
- The Flanders Fields Museum about the First World War
- The city gates: Menenpoort, Rijselpoort, Vismarkt and Vispoort (Menin Gate, Lille Gate, Fish Market and Fish Gate)
- the Kazematten (casemates)
- the Ypres Salient AutoRoute
- the Memorial Museum Passchendaele 1917 in Zonnebeke
- Tyne Cot and the war cemeteries

Tip: every day at 8pm the Last Post ceremony takes place at the Menin Gate in honour of all who died in the First World War.

Toerisme Ieper
Grote Markt 34, B-8900 Ypres
+32(0)57/23 92 20
toerisme@ieper.be
www.toerismeieper.be
www.toerismewesthoek.be

OUDE MAALDERIJ (Brouwfirma d')

Deo Optimo Maximo (DOM), Farang, Hop De Brewer, Leviathan vs The Kraken, Qantelaar, Redenaar

Welcome to a microbrewery complete with specialty beers and shop. Nothing but pure tastes are on offer here. Try a house beer from the tap or a vintage beer. D'Oude Maalderij even brews a Thai triple at the request of a local restaurant serving Thai food. Consider this a warning to your taste buds. The Triporteur beers are also brewed here on behalf of BOM Brewery. Discover a blond and a dark beer, wood-matured or not, where the malt and hop interact beautifully. Or go for an IPA, porter, stout, *imperial stout* or a strong *barley wines* or a *single run*. **TIP:** take your time to look around the café, nothing less than a living beer museum.

Visit by prior arrangement.

Ardooiestraat 130, Izegem
+32(0)486/69 30 34 – doudemaalderij@hotmail.com
www.doudemaalderij.com

OSTEND

Things to see and do
- the marina and fishing port
- the seawall
- the Kursaal and the casino
- the Thermae Palace and the Venetian Galleries
- the Ensor House and its museum
- MuZEE with paintings by Ensor and Spilliaert
- De Grote Post cultural centre
- Fort Napoleon
- the Atlantic Wall open air museum

Tip: visit the annual North Sea Beer Festival during the last weekend of August (see also: beer festivals). www.northseabeerfestival.com

Visit Oostende
Monacoplein 2
B-8400 Oostende
+32(0)59/70 11 99
info@visitoostende.be
www.visitoostende.be

PLUKKER (De)

Keikoppenbier, Rookop, Tripel Plukker, Single Green Hop, All Inclusive IPA

This brewery is owned by the first and only organic hop business in Belgium. Joris Cambie grows eight varieties of aroma hops. 'Organic culture requires extensive natural fertilisation afterwards, and a natural approach to fighting diseases,' he explains. 'Through its very nature, the hop plant is very susceptible to diseases. This can only be expected from a fast-growing climber. Within two months it will grow up to six metres high.' The brewing kettle only contains hop cones produced on the farm. The blond top-fermented beer that goes under the name of Keikop pays homage to the citizens of Poperinge who are said to be 'koppig' or headstrong. Joris: 'I am proud that all my beers are brewed with fresh, green hop cones from my own land. The hop flowers go straight from the vine into the boiling kettle.' The All Inclusive IPA contains all the different varieties of hop grown on the farm. 'In this region we mainly grow English and German aroma hops as well as Cascade and Centennial, which turn out milder here than in the USA', Joris tells us. Besides hop, the farm also grows organic barley for brewing. Joris is the son of a hop farmer. 'Everything is brewed and bottled right here', he assures us. **TIP:** visit the Poperinge hop museum, explore the Westhoek by bike or on foot.

Visits by prior arrangement for 15 and over.

Elverdingseweg 14a, Proven (Poperinge)
+32(0)475/57 36 85 – brouwerij@plukker.be
www.plukker.be

RODENBACH

Rodenbach, Caractère Rouge, Grand Cru, Rosso, Vintage

Rodenbach is still brewed in a splendid 19th century environment. After an initial maturation period taking several weeks the beer is pumped across to one of the 294 oak foeders where it will mature for at least eighteen months. The oldest foeder dates back as far as 1836. Amongst Belgian beers, Rodenbach is a veritable icon. Rudi Ghequire, the master brewer, raves about his beer and this is plain to all. 'So how do we obtain this typical sweet and sour taste? It's all to do with our method of mixed fermentation and the maturation in wooden barrels designed to prolong the storage period of the beer. Local brewers used to allow part of the beer they produced to turn sour in oak barrels. This sour beer would then be added to young beer that had finished fermenting.' Rodenbach is almost entering wine territory. The fishermen at the coast used to think of it as a cheap alternative to white wine. It will come as no surprise that Rodenbach has the same acidity as wine: 3.5 pH. At Rodenbach's the hop bitter is below the taste threshold. 'We only need the hop to produce a stable head on the beer but otherwise you barely notice the taste', Rudi Ghequire continues. 'The beer makes a great pairing with food thanks to the fact that it does not contain any bitterness. This sourish beer gives you an appetite and promotes digestion.' Rodenbach contains several varieties of coloured malts, ground maize for the tender *moelleux* feeling and Belgian hops from Poperinge. Its fruity character is derived from the wood-matured beer. Rodenbach is made with one quarter of old, matured beer and three quarters of young beer. The Grand Cru contains two thirds of old matured and one third of young beer. **TIP:** visit Roeselare and explore the area of the Leie.

Brewery tours available Monday-Thursday for groups comprising 15 to 50. A Rodenbach menu can be enjoyed in the visitors' centre by prior arrangement.

Spanjestraat 133, Roeselare -
+32(0)51/22 34 00 – www.palm.be
www.rodenbach.be
Dienst Bezoeken, Steenhuffeldorp 3, Steenhuffel
+32(0)52/31 74 14 – events@palmbreweries.com
www.palmbreweries.com

ROESELARE

Things to see and do
- the Town Hall and the Market
- the Sint-Michielskerk and its clock tower
- the Wielermuseum (Cycling Museum)
- Michels Filmmuseum
- Rumbeke Castle

Toerisme Roeselare
Delaerestraat 33
B-8800 Roeselare
+32(0)51/26 96 00
www.toerismeroeselare.be

↑ Poperinge, town hall

SEIZOENSBROUWERIJ VANDEWALLE

Reninge Bitter Blond, Reninge Krieken Rood, Reninge Oud Bruin

Chris Vandewalle is the initiator of the smallest home brewery in the Westhoek. Chris, who manages the archives of the city of Diksmuide, sets out to make beers that follow the tradition of regional, seasonal beers. He sources all of his hops from Poperinge. This seasonal brewery produces a Reninge Bitter Blond and a Reninge Oud Bruin. The well-hopped blond seasonal beer is brewed between September and May whereas the oudbruin (old brown) is intended for the winter months. 'I am sticking to the tradition of cut beers (young beer blended with another beer that is one year old). My brown beer will continue to mature in wooden foeders', Chris explains. 'Brewers used to be 'cutters' above all. Take a look at the gueuzestekers who used to blend several different lambics. I have recently 'cut' an Oud Beersel lambic with Reninge Bitter Blond.' **TIP:** visit De Snoek brewery museum (see things to see and do).

Visit by prior arrangement (a maximum of five guests). Opportunity to taste the beer.

> Zwartestraat 43, Reninge
> +32(0)497/54 95 85
> info@seizoensbrouwerij.be
> www.seizoensbrouwerij.be

ST. BERNARDUS

St. Bernardus-range, Watou Tripel

In the early 20th century this brewery developed from a cheese dairy. The St. Bernardus beers have been brewed here ever since 1946. Up until 1992 St. Bernardus produced the beers from the nearby abbey of Sint-Sixtus in Westvleteren under licence, using the traditional recipes. 'Our own beers are doing well, especially the Abt and the new Christmas Ale', the brewer emphasises. He works with spring water with a high mineral content but moderately low in salt in combination with aroma hops from Poperinge. 'Our beers still use the yeast from the abbey of Sint Sixtus', he reveals. This brewery with its own hop fields is just a stone's throw away from the French border. **TIP:** this brewery is a great base for exploring the Westhoek region. Follow the Volkssportroute (popular sports trail), set up at the initiative of the Poperinge Tourist Office.

Visits on request. Stay overnight 'in the brewery' at the Brouwershuis B&B.

> Trappistenweg 23, Watou
> +32(0)57/38 80 21
> visit@sintbernardus.be
> www.sintbernardus.be

POPERINGE

Things to see and do
- the Hop Museum (see things to see and do)
- the Talbot House to gain an insight into daily life away from the frontlines during WWI
- the military cemeteries of the First World War
- the Sint-Janskerk (13th century)
- the statue of Meester Ghybe, a folklore hero
- the sun dial at Burgemeester de Sagherplein
- the variety of walking and cycling routes throughout the Westhoek

Tip: come to the Beer and Hop Festival, held every three years

Toerisme Poperinge
Grote Markt 1
B-8970 Poperinge
+32(0)57/34 66 76
www.toerismepoperinge.be

DAMME

Things to see and do
- The medieval city centre with City Hall and Huyse de Grote Sterre
- Onze-Lieve-Vrouw Hemelvaartkerk
- The Oostkerke Village Mill
- Haringmarkt or Herring market, a tiny picturesque square
- Sint-Christoffelhoeve, the St. Christopher's Farm

Tip: jump on a bike or take a walk through the polders to explore their small villages, also visit Bruges or the North Sea Coast.

Toerisme Damme
Jacob van Maerlantstraat 3
B-8340 Damme – +32(0)50/28 86 10
toerisme@damme.be
www.toerismedamme.be

SIPHON BREWING

Blinker, Cassandra, Damme Nation

Irish lawyer and beer journalist Breándan Kearney got together with brewing engineer Franklin Verdonck to set up a microbrewery in the former sheep barns of the Siphon restaurant at the Damse Vaart canal. They never cease to amaze us with their beers that are rooted in Belgian, Irish and American tradition but always pay homage to the Damme region. The local Leopold and Schipdonk canals are commonly known as 'Blinker' and 'Stinker'. This is why they gave their rather dry Belgian *saison*, in which yeast and citrus aromas play a major role, the name of Blinker. Damme Nation is an amber-coloured American *East Coast IPA* (India Pale Ale) with a lovely balance of hop and malt. Cassandra is named after a mermaid who, according to legend, once entangled a fisherman in his own nets. Oyster shells from the restaurant lend a slightly salty touch to this full-mouthed,

malty oyster stout. Siphon Brewing also produces quirky seasonal beers. **TIP:** taste the beers with a meal in the Siphon house restaurant (www.siphon.be) and order oysters, smoked eel or coq au vin.

Damse Vaart-Oost 1, Damme
+32(0)50/62 02 02 – www.siphonbrewing.be

STRUBBE

De Couckelaerschen Doedel, Dikke Mathilde, Edel-Brau, Ichtegem's Grand Cru, Houten Kop, Keyte, Kriekenbier, Oud Bier, Strubbe Pils, Vlas Kop, Wittoen

In 1830 Carolus Strubbe left Tielt to try his luck in Ichtegem. He became a farmer as well as a brewer. During the summer months he was working in the fields and when the winter arrived, he could be found on the malt floor as well as wielding the mashing stick. In those days brewers grew their own ingredients. These included barley and other grains but hops were also cultivated in various locations. The barrels and basins were crafted or repaired by the brewery itself. This artisan approach explains why barrels differ in size and capacity. Ever since its foundation, the brewery has remained in the hands of the Strubbe family and has passed from father to son for six generations. Strubbe is one of the last remaining breweries to produce a sour Flemish ale. Ichtegem's Grand Cru yields amazing aromas of caramel, cherries and balsamic vinegar coupled with a refreshingly sour, fruity and malty taste with impressions of wood. Beer stored for two years in oak barrels, soured in the natural way, is blended with a sweeter, top-fermented beer. De Keyte Dobbel Tripel pairs candy sugar with roast malt. **TIP:** sample the beers in café De Vlasschaard in Stene on the outskirts of Ostend (www.devlasschaard.be).

Get in touch with the brewery to arrange your visit.

Markt 1, Ichtegem – +32(0)51/58 81 16
info@brouwerij-strubbe.be
www.brouwerij-strubbe.be

STRUISE BROUWERS (De)

AJ, Black Albert, Black Damnation, Cuvée Delphine, Elliot, Five Squared, Havic, Imperialist, Kabert, Macadame, Our Nastiest Effort, Pannepot, Struise Witte, Tjeeses, Ypres

In 2008, ratebeer.com awarded a couple of chaps from Woesten the accolade of the best brewers in the world. You can taste their beers in a former village school in Oostvleteren. De Struise Brouwers established their reputation with strong beers, in particular with De Pannepot, their flagship beer. We are talking about a jet-black degustation beer with a frothy, milky head and aromas of coffee, chocolate and brioche or raisin bread. 'We were brought up with the strong abbey beers popular in the area, especially the Westvleteren Abt', Carlo Grootaert tells us. 'We grew to appreciate them and so we built up our taste memory.' Brewer Urbain Coutteau chips in: 'You learn on the job and that shows in the glass. When we started out we used three hop varieties. We are now using thirty-five, all different.' The range comprises 'outsider' beers: extremely bitter brews as well as wood-matured beers and barley wines. **TIP:** taste the beers in 't Molenhof (www.t-molenhof.be) only a stone's throw away from the brewery.

This brewery welcomes you every Saturday afternoon. Tasting sessions are held as part of beer education.

Kasteelstraat 50, Oostvleteren
+32(0)495/28 86 23
struisesales@gmail.com
www.struise.com

TOYE (Brouwerij)

Goedendag

This beer is named after the heavy club that was swung by knights to beat their enemies to a pulp. Fortunately, the beer is a lot more subtle than the 'say Hello' from the olden days. The brewer finds that his dark Goedendag makes a great pairing with the cheese of the same name. Who are we to contradict him?

Visit by prior arrangement.

Rekkemsestraat 64, Marke, Kortrijk
+32(0)498/39 37 11
info@goedendagbier.be
www.goedendagbier.be

VAN EECKE

Hommelbier, Kapittel, Leroy Christmas, Watou's Wit

In 1692 the status of the Yedegem dynasty from Watou was elevated to that of Counts. The family owned a castle and a brewery. Both buildings were razed to the ground at the time of the French Revolution. It was only the brewery that rose from the ashes. A question of priorities... The buildings were acquired by Van Eecke in 1862. Initially only top-fermented beers were produced but abbey beers were added to the range after the Second World War. Hommelbier is the flagship beer. Where does the name come from? The Westhoek area around Poperinge has a tradition of hop cultivation, 'hommel' in local dialect. The 'Poperingse' Hommelbier was inspired by the Hoppestoet parade. This golden-coloured beer with its robust collar of froth and delicate aroma of hop bitters pays homage to the noble hop plant. Also in 1862 and through marriage, Van Eecke became the owner of Het Sas brewery in Boezinge, now the producer of several local top-fermented beers as well as the popular Sas Pils. **TIP:** enjoy the beers at Het Brouwershof right next to the brewery or else in beer restaurant 't Hommelhof at the market square.

You can only visit this village brewery by appointment.

Brouwerij Van Eecke, Douvieweg 2, Watou
+32(0)457/38 80 30 of +32(0)57/42 20 05
info@brouwerijvaneecke.be
www.brouwerijvaneecke.be
www.hommelbier.be

VAN HONSEBROUCK (Castle Brewery)

Bacchus, Barista, Brigand, Cuvée du Chateau, Filou, Kasteel-range, St-Louis-range, Slurfke, Trignac XII

When Luc Van Honsebrouck joined the brewery in 1953 it was producing brown table beer, export beer, pils and an old brown (which was to become Bacchus). In 1955 Luc decided to stop production of pils. Meanwhile, Bacchus turned into a success. In 1957 Luc purchased twenty tonnes of lambic wort permeated by wild yeasts from the valley of the Senne. He blended the lambic with fresh wort and fermented this mixture in wooden barrels. And thus the Gueuze St. Louis was born, to be followed by a kriek and a raspberry beer. Later on, Van Honsebrouck introduced draught gueuze. An interesting bit of trivia is that a 'gueuze war' was raging in Belgian football throughout the 1970s. Van Honsebrouck sponsored Club Bruges with its St. Louis fruit beers, whereas Anderlecht wore the name of Vanderstock's Belle-Vue on its shirts. Sparks flew on the football pitch and in the local hostelries. The demand for heavy, blond beers increased throughout the 1980s. In response, Van Honsebrouck launched the Brigand, a malted, strong and heavy beer. Brigand was the name given to the farmers of Ingelmunster who revolved against the 'sans culottes' (the nickname given to French soldiers) in 1798 in the nearby village of Hulste. The strong Kasteelbier – Kasteel for short – came onto the market after the brewer had purchased Ingelmunster Castle. Tasting a few bottles of old Kasteel inspired him to produce a gastronomic beer. Kasteel's touches of port and Madeira prompted the introduction of Cuvée du Château. There is also the Trignac XII, which is a Kasteel Tripel matured in barrels previously used for cognac. The jet-black Barista, successor to Kasteel Winter, builds a bridge between beer and coffee whereas Kasteel Rouge, a blend of Kasteel Donker and cherry liqueur, is one of the strongest fruit beers on the market. The brewer has also returned to the roots of lambic beers with his unsweetened St. Louis Fond Tradition Gueuze and Kriek. The dark Slurfke is based on the beer brewed by Eddy Van Noteghem, a character from the popular TV soap *Thuis*. You could say that in this case, truth has overtaken fiction. **TIP:** taste the beers at café Lagaar at Izegem railway station and take the next train home, or the one after that… If you are in Antwerp, pop into Bar Filou at Grand Café De Rooden Hoed (www.deroodenhoed.be), the smallest bar 'van 't stad'.

Brouwerij Van Honsebrouck recently moved from Ingelmunster, its base for over a century, to the nearby town of Izegem. Het Bierkasteel is a brand new, state-of-the-art brewery of specialty beers, its cafés and restaurants well-equipped to welcome visitors. Take a tour of the imposing brewhall, bottling plant, barrel hall and foeder chamber. The brewery is also an excellent venue for meetings and parties.

Ingelmunstersestraat 80, Emelgem (Izegem)
+32(0)51/33 51 60 – www.vanhonsebrouck.be

↑ Damse vaart

VERHAEGHE-VICHTE

Barbe, Cambrinus, Christmas Verhaeghe, Duchesse de Bourgogne, Echt Kriekenbier, Verhaeghe Pils, Vichtenaar

This brewery presents a striking blend of the old and the new. Verhaeghe-Vichte started trading in 1885. Some of its equipment dates back to the late 19th century: the malt tower with malt floor, the steeping basins and germination floors, the storage lofts and the free-standing factory chimney. The brewhall was constructed in the 1970s. Some of this brewery's foeders are over eighty years old. A range of younger, oak foeders take pride of place in a new extension. The foeders are used to mature sour Flemish red-brown ales: Barbe Ruby, Duchesse de Bourgogne and Vichtenaar. **TIP:** the area is perfect for cycling. The local cycling network (Fietsnetwerk Leiestreek) connects canals and disused railway tracks with the cities and cuts across the hilly, green land of the Leie and the Scheldt. Phone ahead to arrange your visit.

Sint-Dierikserf 1, Vichte – +32(0)56 77 70 32
www.brouwerijverhaeghe.be

VERZET (Brouwers)

Golden Tricky, Moose Blues, Oakey Moakey Whisky Stout, Oud Bruin, Super NoAH, Rebel Local

'Ons goesting doen' is Flemish for 'We're doing whatever we feel like doing'. The brewing virus has these brewers in its grip. Koen Van Lanker and his brothers-in-arms Jordan and Alex create a bit of rock-'n-roll magic in the glass. They learnt all the ins-and-outs of their profession at De Ranke, Gulden Spoor and Toye. Brewer Koen earned his spurs at De Proefbrouwerij. 'We are making traditional beers that are just that little bit different', Koen laughs. Bring to mind a hoppy triple, a double with maple syrup, a wood-matured 'cut beer' of the old brown variety, a light 'session beer' with plenty of taste, made with Belgian hops, and an aromatic single hop IPA. These gentlemen have a veritable thirst for experimenting. They invite colleagues to brew at Brouwers Verzet and like to take up a *co-brewing* challenge. From time to time the standard range is enhanced by one-off, idiosyncratic bootlegs. Discover the taste of an old brown beer with fruit infusions added or how Anzegem has put its own dot on the beer map. **TIP:** taste the beers at Café Local, the café owned by the brewery. Tours for groups of five and over by prior arrangement.

Brouwers Verzet, Grote Leiestraat 117, Anzegem
+32(0)470/17 06 34 – +32(0)474/81 79 05
info@brouwersverzet.be
www.brouwersverzet.be

WESTVLETEREN (Sint-Sixtusabdij)

Westvleteren 6, 8 en 12

At the In de Vrede abbey café the world-renowned Westvleteren beers are poured freshly from the bottle. Aromas of caramel, coffee, grapes, prunes, mild spices with a touch of vanilla, a hint of barley, with a high alcohol content and at the same time very subtle... Westvleteren, as always, is bravely resisting the pressure of market forces. The abbot is not yielding, even by an inch. The monks are brewing 75 days a year and not a day more. Westvleteren is like a drop of holy water in a sea of beer. This beer is worth its weight in gold on eBay. The best beer in the world? Or just impossible to track down? **TIP:** follow the Sint-Sixtus walking trail (7 or 10km), visit one of the two hundred-plus war cemeteries from the First World War or the In Flanders Fields Museum in Ypres. If you'd rather stick to beer, the Poperinge Hop Museum is well worth visiting.

No, neither this Trappist abbey nor its brewery are open to the public. Enjoy a beer and a bite to eat in the abbey tavern called In De Vrede, where you can also lay your hands on a few bottles of Trappist beer. Wander around the virtual museum about abbey life.

Donkerstraat 13, Westvleteren
+32(0)57/40 03 77 – info@indevrede.be
www.indevrede.be

THINGS TO SEE AND DO

BROUWERIJMUSEUM DE SNOEK
Mout- en Brouwhuis De Snoek (maltings and brewing house) is a unique museum with a construction based on the tried-and-trusted cascade system. From the loft right the way down to the cellar, visitors learn all there is to know about the entire malting and brewing process in the early 19th century. The explanation is provided by the vintage equipment on display: copper brew kettles, a cast-iron mashing basin, centuries old fermentation basins and barrels, a malthouse remarkably still intact, a vintage gas-driven engine, and so forth. You will be told the story of thirst in the Great War and follow in the footsteps of the soldiers who fought at the front. Your tour finishes at the old inn of Het Brouwershof, now completely restored, where you can sample the Snoekbier. **TIP:** pop into museum café Het Brouwershof and enjoy the range of specialty beers on offer.

Fortem 40, Alveringem – +32(0)58/28 96 74
infomuseum@desnoek.be -www.desnoek.be

BRUGES BEER MUSEUM
Come to this museum, overlooked by the belfry, to discover the rich history of beer in Belgium and Bruges in particular. Armed with an iPad, click on the QR code when you come across a particular object and its entire story is at your fingertips. Many important topics are highlighted: beer and health, women and beer, beer styles, to name but a few. Take part in the quiz to test your beer knowledge. There is a tour specially aimed at children, illustrated with beautiful pictures. In the loft there is a display of brewing equipment. Brewing processes and the use of raw ingredients in large oak foeders will also be explained and you will learn the secrets of Trappist beers. Before, during or after your visit you will taste typical Bruges beers or else the beers made by Palm Belgian Craft Brewers, including the unfiltered Palm and the foeder beers made by Rodenbach and the Boon lambic brewery. Ask if there is anything 'special' on offer. If you're lucky, there may be a test brew from microbrewery De Hoorn, owned by Palm Belgian Craft Brewers, or else a zesty version of Bruges Tripel.

Breidelstraat 3, Bruges – +32(0)50/69 92 29
info@brugesbeermuseum.com
www.brugesbeermuseum.com

HOPMUSEUM POPERINGE
The Hop Museum is housed in the former "Stadsschaal" building, otherwise known as the Municipal Scales. This is where hops used to be weighed, quality checked and stacked in large bags. Hop flowers were dried just underneath the roof of the farm before being bagged and compressed by the feet of the 'bagger'. The hop museum manages an extensive collection of vintage hop processing equipment, complemented by audio-visual material and various quizzes to test your knowledge. This contemporary museum focuses on the history and the life cycle of the hop plant. It turns out that not many people are familiar with hops. The brewers use unfertilised – female – hop cones which contain the lupuline agent that helps to preserve the beer. Hop also gives the beer its bitterness and aromas. The soil in this region is made up of loam and sand on a water-retaining base of clay. It has proved eminently suitable for hop cultivation. During the Middle Ages the cities of Ypres and Poperinge were engaged in competition for the linen trade. Under pressure of the City of Ypres the Count of Flanders put a stop to the linen trade in Poperinge. In later years, thanks to the French abbey of Saint-Omer in France, hops were grown as an alternative crop to flax.

Gasthuisstraat 71, 8970 Poperinge
+32(0)57/33 79 22 – hopmuseum@poperinge.be
www.hopmuseum.be

WESTTOER
Koning Albert I-laan 120
B-8200 Sint-Michiels Bruges
+32(0)50 30 55 00
info@westtoer.be
www.westtoer.be

BRUSSELS
HALLE
LEUVEN
LOUVAIN-LA-NEUVE
NIVELLES
WATERLOO
WAVRE

AB INBEV (Stella Artois)

Stella Artois, Leffe

Stella Artois first saw the light in 1926 when it was launched as a Christmas beer. It has now developed into the best known Belgian pils beer with yeast still based on the cells first grown in 1926. This brewery, the largest one in Europe, is now producing 12 million hectolitres every year. 'The brewhall comprises four production lines that can work completely independently from each other', our guide tells us. 'The kettles in the brewhall extend upwards to over two floors. The narrow pipes that feed into the barrels contain the ingredients for the beer. The wide pipes are used to disperse the steam produced by the brewing process. This steam accounts for the typical Stella smell you can sniff in Louvain if the wind comes in from the right direction.' The tour gives an overview of the brewhall as it used to be and shows you what it looks like now. The operators, glued to their screens, used to scrape off the yeast that was floating on the top of the fermentation tank. Everything is now done at the push of a button. A large proportion of the beers produced are destined for export. Stella Artois is not the only beer brewed here. The Leffe range – with the exception of the Triple and the Royale – also comes from AB Inbev. 'At every stage of the brewing process we conduct tastings. We will taste the wort, the brewing water, the water used for processing, the beer in cold storage...', the brewer assures us. The brewing process takes up six-and-a-half hours followed by a period of ten to twelve days during which the beer ferments, goes into cold storage, is filtered and bottled or used to fill barrels. So, does the beer taste better on tap or from the bottle? 'The pils tastes best from the tap, provided the pipes are rinsed regularly and that the beer is poured as it should be.' The brewer explains that the water comes from thirty different wells spread across the city. Each main beer has its own yeast which contributes to the taste, together with the (pils) malt and the European hops. 'The quality of the malt is different for every batch harvested and also between different harvest years. We have to remain watchful at all times. At the end of the day, the customer expects the same taste in the glass but the ingredients will vary all the time.' **TIP:** visit the historic Stella Artois brewhall, the De Hoorn microbrewery (see further on) and the brewery buildings around the Vaartkom, a former industrial site that is now being re-developed into a hub for living, shopping and simply browsing.

Explore Europe's largest brewery. Visits available for groups of 15 and over from Tuesday to Saturday. Book your visit at www.breweryvisits.com where you will find a range of options.

Brouwerijplein 1, Louvain (Leuven)
+32(0)16/24 71 11 – www.ab-inbev.com

Brouwerij De Hoorn, founded in 1923, is the birthplace of Stella Artois. This imposing building is included in the monument register, mainly thanks to its impressive 'Artois' brewhall and the unique way in which it was constructed. Stella Artois saw the light here in 1926. Several rooms in this historic building are equipped to teach visitors about the history and importance of De Hoorn, all within a modern setting. The De Hoorn microbrewery has its own Stella Artois Flagship Café.

Sluisstraat 79, Louvain (Leuven)
+32(0)4585/16 90 24 – www.dehoorn.eu

AFFLIGEM BROUWERIJ

Affligem, Op-Ale

In 1129, 67 years after its foundation, the Affligem abbey brewery first appeared in official records. Throughout their lives, the monks of Affligem stuck to a strict regime of eight hours' work, eight hours of prayer and eight hours of rest. The history of this abbey was quite tumultuous, however. On 11th November 1796, at the time of the French Revolution, the abbey buildings were destroyed and its lands were confiscated. The monks only returned in 1869. They established themselves in the baroque-style Bishops' Residence that had escaped the vagaries of the war. The brothers set up a new brewery in 1885 and in 1970 their recipes were re-acquired by Brouwerij De Smedt in Opwijk, which was later called Affligem Brouwerij. The brewhall was constructed just after the Second World War. Op-Ale-amber beer follows the tradition of the *spéciale belge*. It is made with a yeast culture that originates in England. 'We harvest the yeast from the top and re-use it', the brewer reveals. Monks introduced hops to the region. In the 17th century Aalst and its surroundings accounted for over half of all the hop grown in Europe. After 1950 hop imports from Eastern Europe took over from the regionally grown hops. Nowadays this climber is growing once again in Aalst, Asse and Affligem.

The brewery is closed to the public.
If you wish to visit the abbey, please get in touch with ben.vermoesen@telenet.be.

Brouwerij, Ringlaan 18b, Opwijk
+32(0)52/35 99 11 – www.affligembeer.be
Abdij, Abdijstraat 6, Affligem
+32(0)53/66 70 25 – www.abdijaffligem.be

ANGERIK

Dilleke

Sam Decuyper operates this microbrewery in Dilbeek on the edge of Brussels. Taste Dilleke, a pale ale from Dilbeek.

Visitors welcome on Saturdays between 1200 and 1600.

Snakkaertstraat 30, Dilbeek
+32(0)477/37 15 86 – info@angerik.be

AVERBODE

Averbode, Momentum

In the completely renovated abbey barn an abbey café was established. You can see the stainless steel brewing kettles from behind a glass wall. You find yourself in the visitors' centre Het Moment, which comprises a brewery as well as a bakery, cheese dairy and shop. The experience centre provides further information on abbey life and tourist destinations in the region in general. Momentum abbey beer is an unfiltered thirstquencher with a great head of froth. The nose picks up amazing aromas of malt and hop with an subtle hint of sweet fruits. All is beautifully balanced, with a mild bitterness, a sweet fruitiness and impressions of almond and caramel. Momentum matures for three weeks before being transferred to the pouring tank with its direct connection to the bar tap. **TIP:** Averbode is an excellent destination for walkers, cyclists and horse riders. The abbey is located on a newly opened hike and bike trail not far from Hoeve Den Eik and its Clog Museum.

Het Moment Visitors' Centre is located in a beautifully restored barn within the grounds of the abbey. The barn also houses a microbrewery. Open from Tuesday – Sunday.

Abdijstraat 1 (Herseltsebaan 2), Averbode
+32(0)13/78 04 40 – abdij@abdijaverbode.be
www.averbodia.be
www.averbodemoment.be

BEERSTORMING

You won't find a standard beer menu here. Rather, you are invited to attend a convivial brewing session under the watchful eye of Antoine Lavis, an agricultural engineer. At a *beerstorm*, five to 14 attendees decide in democratic fashion on what will be flowing out of the tanks in due course. The tasting includes five brews produced at previous beerstorming sessions. In only a few weeks' time you can pick up your own beer.

Alsembergsesteenweg 75, Brussels
+32(0)472/89 74 01
www.beerstorming.net

BELGOOBEER

Belgoo

Jo Van Aert brews at a former drinks' store on the outskirts of Brussels. This brewer specialises in multi-grain beers and uses barley as well as spelt, oats and wheat. The beers are quite hoppy, thanks also to the use of *dry hopping* during cold storage. **TIP:** visit the Pajottenland region and the valley of the Senne, the birthplace of lambic beers.

Contact the brewery to make arrangements for your visit.

Georges Wittouckstraat 61, Sint-Pieters-Leeuw
+32(0)475/69 24 60
info@belgoobeer.com
www.belgoobeer.com

Averbode, abbey

↓ Nivelles, Sint-Gertrudischurch

BELGO SAPIENS BREWERS

Blanche de Thines, Colonel Arch, Polarius, P'tit Granit

This microbrewery set up shop in an industrial area on the outskirts of Namur. Damien Demunter, Frédéric Delsaut and Mathieu Lainé brew pils, white beer, amber beer and porter. Their trade mark: light beers brewed with aroma hops; no herbs, spices or aromatic agents added. **TIP:** sight-seeing in the historic city centre of Namur or a tour of the Waterloo battlefield.

Visit by prior arrangement.

> Rue du Travail 5, Nivelles
> +32(0)67/33 99 17 – contact@belgosapiens.be
> www.belgosapiens.be

BELLE-VUE

Belle-Vue

The Brussels community of Anderlecht acquired global fame thanks to the Belle-Vue gueuze and kriek produced by the Vanden Stock brewery. This family invested heavily in the well-known Anderlecht football club. The beer is named after a former café purchased by Philemon Vanden Stock, a brewer, in 1927. Philemon laid the basis for the current brewery in 1913. Belle-Vue is made with a standard brew that is pumped into the horizontal wooden 'pijpen' barrels (600 l) and foeders (containing up to 60 hl), where it continues to ferment through contact with the ambient air. 'We don't use an open cooling basin as we want to be in complete charge of the process', the brewer states. 'The microflora within the barrels determines the taste. This is why we work with barrels previously used for red port. The quality and quantity of the bacteria in the barrel make all the difference.' Belle-Vue is produced on the basis of lambic that is between nine and fifteen months old. The kriek is made with whole cherries from the Tienen area.

This former brewery on a Brussels canal is now home to a three-star hotel and a contemporary art museum. AB Inbev closed this facility in 2006 and moved production to Sint-Pieters-Leeuw, a site that is not open to visitors.

> Monssesteenweg 144, Sint-Pieters-Leeuw
> www.ab-inbev.com

BLOCK (De)

Dendermonde, Kastaar, Réservée De Block, Satan, Sint-Timotheus

This story originates in the 14th century when Henricus De Block acquired the rights to brew for the Duke of Brabant. The history of this brewery has been carefully preserved, treasured and polished to a shine and is now on display in two reception rooms joined by colourful posters and pictures on the walls. Discover how things were done in the olden days: bottling, corking and producing natural corks. Also admire a collection of vintage bottles, glasses and other paraphernalia. **TIP:** visit Meise Horticultural Gardens or the Atomium.

Microbrewery with brewery museum in an ancient farm. Discover a wide-ranging display of ancient brewing technology. Group visits to be arranged in advance.

> Nieuwbaan 92, Peizegem-Merchtem
> +32(0)52/37 21 59
> www.satanbeer.com

HALLE

Things to see and do
- Sint-Maartensbasiliek
- the City Hall and the central market square
- Den Ast, the former Van Roye malt works (+32(0)2/365 97 70)
- Hallerbos forest and its Bosmuseum

Tip: visit the Hallerbos in spring when the bluebells are in flower

Toerisme Halle, Pajottenland & Zennevallei
Grote Markt 1
1500 Halle
+32(0)2/356 42 59
http://www.toerisme-pajottenland.be/

BOON

Oude Geuze Boon, Geuze Mariage Parfait, Kriek Boon, Oude Kriek Boon, Kriek Mariage Parfait, Framboise Boon, Faro Boon

The history of this brewery goes all the way back to 1680 when the Claes family established a brewery at their farm in Lembeek. Frank Boon has been wielding the mashing stick ever since 1978 when he acquired the ailing De Vits brewery. Frank Boon has been instrumental in ensuring legal protection for the Old Gueuze beer style, in collaboration with Jacques Van Cutsem (Timmermans), André De Keersmaeker (Mort Subite) and Jacques De Keersmaeker (Belle-Vue). At the end of the 1960s he experienced the fledgling renaissance of specialty beers. Today, Lembeek is home to a plethora of oak foeders where all in all, over a million litres of lambic mature. This brewery is a supplier of lambic to 'gueuzestekers' and produces its own classic Oude Geuze and Oude Kriek as well as a very popular Kriek. The lambic is cold stored in oak barrels. To this end, the Boon brewery has a large area comprising over one hundred horizontal foeders that each contain eight thousand litres on average. These foeders were purchased from European brewers and winemakers over the years. Only aged oak is suitable as new oak contains too many tannins, which makes it unsuitable for beer. The oak lets in just the right amount of oxygen needed for the development of the wild yeasts. This spontaneous fermentation produces the very finest gueuze. Each foeder, filled up to the brim, has its own character and influences the taste in its own unique way. Gueuze and kriek that are produced in the correct, traditional manner are ready to drink half a year after bottling but can be stored for twenty years or more. 'The wild yeasts age the contents of the bottle in a positive way', Frank Boon assures us. He strives to produce a gueuze of consistent quality. Brouwerij Boon has made investments in the first fully automated lambic brewery. Brewing can be done continuously in the new brewhall; up to four brews a day. Producing lambic takes a lot of time. Frank Boon follows the 'trouble wort method' which uses 40% unmalted wheat. 'We are brewing a beer that gains in taste and character after six months and that is very complex. Also, we are still making use of the traditional filtration basin to make sure the lambic preserves its individual character. The current open cooling basin will remain operational, too', Frank assures us. A successful marriage between the old and the new, that much is evident. **TIP:** a great starting point for sightseeing in Hallen and the Pajottenland area.

Get in touch with Toerisme Halle to book your visit: +32(0)2/356 42 59 – www.toerisme-halle.be

> Fonteinstraat 65, Lembeek (Halle)
> +32(0)2/356 66 44
> info@boon.be www.boon.be

BRABANT
(La Brasserie du)

La Brabançonne, La Moche de Noël,
La Cuvée Nico

Farm-based craft brewery in Baisy-Thy. Visit by prior arrangement.

> Rue Banterlez 59, Baisy-Thy
> +32(0)67/79 18 79
> labrasseriedubrabant@skynet.be
> http://users.skynet.be/labrasseriedubrabant/

BRASSE-TEMPS (Le)

Ambrasse-Temps, Blanche de Ste Waudru,
Brasse-Temps, Bush, Cuvée des Trolls, Surfine

Le Brasse-Temps serves the house beers Cuvée des Trolls, Ambrasse-Temps, Blanche, Brasse-Temps des Cerises, Brasse-Temps Citron and Temps des Brunes as well as the Bush beers produced by Brasserie Dubuisson in their Tournai microbrewery. The four-beer *Rafale* is popular with students.

OTTIGNIES/LOUVAIN-LA-NEUVE EN WAVER

Things to see and do
- the Town Hall and Wavre's historic centre
- the Basilica of Notre-Dame de Basse-Wavre
- Genval Lake
- the ancient square farmhouses of Brabant province, nestled amongst the fields
- the student town of Louvain-la-Neuve
- the Hergé Museum dedicated to the creator of Tintin
- Louvain-la-Neuve Municipal Museum with its art collection

Tourisme Louvain-la-Neuve
Place de l'Université, Gallerie des Halles
B-1348 Louvain-la-Neuve
+32(0)10/47 47 47
info@tourisme-olln.be
www.tourisme-olln.be

Tourisme Wavre
Rue de Nivelles 1
B-1300 Wavre
+32(0)10/23 03 23
info@mtab.be
www.mtab.be

You choose four beers with a different taste and alcohol content. You build up from light to strong and choose a small or large 'Tour infernale'. The more beer you drink, the louder the music is played. **TIP:** visit Louvain-la-Neuve, the youngest city in the country, and the Hergé Museum.

Get in touch with the brewery to arrange your visit.

> Place des Brabançons 4, Louvain-la-Neuve
> +32(0)10/45 70 27
> www.brassetemps.be

BRUSSELSS BEER PROJECT

Babylone, Dark Sister, Delta, Grosse Bertha

'Leave the abbey, join the playground!' is the motto of this craft brewery located in trendy Dansaertstraat right in the heart of Brussels. These up-and-coming *craft brewers* are only too happy to swap tradition for experiment. They are planning to conjure up twenty different brews from their tanks each year to complement their tried-and-trusted beer quartet. Taste them in the brewery café at the top of the street. **TIP:** visit the uber-hip Dansaertstraat, the Halles Saint-Géry (Sint-Gorikshallen) exhibition centre and the Vismarkt (Fish Market).

Open every Thursday, Friday and Saturday between 1400 and 2200.

Dansaertstraat 188
keepintouch@beerproject.be
www.beerproject.be

CAM (De)

De Cam Frambozenbier, Oude Geuze, Kriekenlambiek, Oude Kriek

Gueuzestekerij De Cam is located in a building that was known as 'des Heeres Landcamme' in 1515. 'Cam' means 'brewery' in Old Dutch. The wort is purchased from local lambic brewers. The lambic ferments and matures in wooden barrels until the gueuzesteker approves of the taste. To produce his Oude Geuze he blends the young lambic, matured for at least one year, with a lambic that is at least two years old. The beer continues to mature after bottling. Gueuzesteker Karel Goddeau's other job is that of a brewmaster at Slaghmuylder's in Ninove. 'Really, I'm not doing a lot at De Cam's', he laughs. 'All I do is make sure that my employees can do their work in the best possible conditions.' His employees: the millions of micro-organisms, the *Brettanomyces bruxellensis* and *Brettanomyces lambicus* for example. The work of a gueuzesteker is similar to that of a whisky blender or a champagne 'composer'. In the same way that wine is turned into a sparkling wine, lambic turns into old gueuze after three years' fermentation. The legislator is becoming increasingly aware of the value of old lambic and gueuze. Legal protection will be tightened up in the near future. This means that lambic can only be produced in wooden barrels; it has to result from spontaneous fermentation, cool down in an open cooling basin or 'koelschip' and be delivered unpasteurised and unsweetened. **TIP:** we recommend this region to cyclists and mountain bikers. It has everything you could ever want.

De Cam has links to a community centre with a café where everyone receives a warm welcome. A great venue for tasting regional dishes and discovering traditional and popular café games. A musical instrument museum is located on the first floor. Open every Sunday between 1400 and 1700 with the exception of Bank Holidays and pre-arranged tours. Guided tours available. Visit the gueuzestekerij on request.

Dorpsstraat 67A, Gooik – +32(0)2/532 21 32 of
+32(0)476/81 68 06 – www.lambic.info

CANTILLON

100% Bio, Belgische vlag, Geuze, Grand Cru Bruocsella, Iris, Kriek, Rosé de Gambrinus, Vigneronne, Saint Lamvinus, Fou'Foune, Lou Pepe

Cantillon, a craft lambic brewery, only produces a modest amount of lambic. However, its image and reputation go far above and beyond that. Cantillon is struggling to meet demand. 'To up sticks is not really an option,' Jean-Pierre Van Roy, the brewer, explains. 'This building plays an important role in the spontaneous fermentation process.' Microflora from wild yeasts and other fermentation agents float around in the air. Though invisible, they permeate the wort, multiply thanks to the sugars from the wort and produce alcohol and aromatic components in this way. Cantillon, the last remaining Brussels craft brewery to produce lambic, has turned into a pilgrimage destination for beer lovers. Jean-Pierre Van Roy loves a very dry lambic. The older vintages contain little or no carbon dioxide and are reminiscent of a *fino sherry*. Jean-Pierre uses various types of wood for his barrels, including some that have been used for storing port. Sample the beer and you find that the tart taste in the glass takes some getting used to. Lambics evolve in the bottle. 'Just recently I opened a gueuze that was bottled in 1975. It was absolutely fine, not a trace of sugar', Jean-Pierre tells us. His gueuze is now maturing in bottles in cellars below the Hooikaai in Brussels. Jean-Pierre: 'These famous micro-organisms from the valley of the Senne, *Brettanomyces bruxellensis* and *Brettanomyces lambicus* remain active for years, lending even more character and structure to the beer. They provide the characteristic toasted aromas but even after twenty or thirty years, the taste remains pure and fresh.' **TIP:** combine with a visit to Brussels.

Visit the brewery when production is in progress. Group visits to be arranged in advance.

Gheudestraat 56, Brussels – +32(0)2/521 49 28
info@cantillon.be – www.cantillon.be

BRUSSELS

Things to see and do
- the Grote Markt/Grand Place with its City Hall, the facades of the merchants' houses, including the splendid Brewer's House with its Brewery Museum
- Manneken Pis with or without one of his seven hundred outfits
- Dansaertstraat and the trendy Sint-Gorikshallen/Halles St. Géry area
- the Vismarkt/Marché aux Poissons for its cafés and restaurants
- the Musical Instruments Museum in the former Old England department store built in art nouveau style
- the Marollenwijk area at the bottom of the imposing Court of Justice with the daily flea market at Vossenplein (place du Jeu de Balle)
- the Grote Zavel (Grand Sablon), a Mecca for antiquarians and chocolatiers
- the Jubelpark (Parc du Cinquantenaire) with AutoWorld, the Royal Museum of the Armed Forces and Military History and the Cinquantenaire Museum
- the Royal Museums of Fine Arts with its collections of ancient and modern art
- Place Royale and the Magritte Museum
- BOZAR, the museum of contemporary art
- The Belgian Comic Strip Centre housed in an art nouveau building
- the art nouveau mansions built by Horta and his students, dotted around the city
- Elsene (Ixelles) Museum, the Flagey building and the Vijvers van Elsene (Etangs d'Ixelles)
- the Atomium; the highest sphere of this atom, enlarged 165 billion times, affords a splendid panorama across the city
- the extensive Zoniënbos (Sonian Forest) with its numerous parks and gardens

Tip: visit the annual Belgian Beer Weekend held at the Grand Place during the first weekend of September. www.belgianbrewers.be

Visit Brussels
Koningstraat 2/2 rue Royale, B-1000 Brussels
+32(0)2/513 89 40
www.visitbrussels.be

← Brussels, market square

↑ Brussels, market square

↓ Brussels, market square

DOMUS
(Huisbrouwerij)

Con Domus, Nen Engel, Nostra Domus

Brewing activity in Louvain goes all the way back to the Middle Ages. When clean drinking water was hard to come by, the locals or 'Leuvenaren' would drink beer. This small city was home to hundreds of home breweries, where beer came in all colours, shapes and sizes. Domus is carrying on this tradition. In 1982 Cyriel Roten set up his home brewery in the city. From the brewery the beer literally flows straight into the café. You won't find it any fresher. The first mouthful of Con Domus is bitter with a strong taste of hops. Cyriel laughs: 'All beers used to taste like this. But the big brands have adjusted their pils to fit the taste of the Coca-Cola generation. This beer has twice the amount of bitters compared to your standard pils.' **TIP:** visit the beer city of Leuven.

Brewery tours are held every day except Mondays, between the hours of 1000 and 2000. By appointment only for groups of eight and over.

Tiensestraat 8, Leuven
+32(0)16/20 14 49 – info@domusleuven.be
www.domusleuven.be

---

3 FONTEINEN

Beersel, Doesjel, 3 Fonteinen, Zwet.be

Armand De Belder, a lambic brewer with 3 Fonteinen, insists on his individuality: he creates and produces just what he fancies doing. This lambic brewer and 'gueuzesteker' pays attention to every detail and searches obsessively for natural ingredients and the most suitable methods. Armand enjoys an international reputation thanks to his expertise in brewing lambic, old gueuze and kriek. His father Gaston taught him all there is to know about lambic.

This artisan lambic brewery and 'gueuzestekerij' oozes tradition from every pore. Group tours (for 10 – 30 visitors) are held every Friday and Saturday. Individuals and smaller groups are welcome one Saturday each month (refer to the website for dates). Taste the beers with or without a bite to eat in the 3 Fonteinen house restaurant. The beer experience centre Lambik-O-droom, based in Lot, is set to open in early 2017 with a tasting room, restaurant and shop. From then on, lambic will mature on the banks of the river Senne. Cherry trees of the Schaarbeekse krieken variety will be planted. The brewery itself will remain in Beersel.

Hoogstraat 2a, Beersel
+32(0)2/306 71 03 of +32(0)495/54 06 52
info@3fonteinen.be
www.3fonteinen.be
Molenstraat 47, Lot
lambikodroom@3fonteinen.be

LEUVEN (LOUVAIN)

Things to see and do
- the Gothic City Hall and the market square
- the Grand and Small Beguinages
- Sint-Pieterskerk and its treasures
- the abbeys of Park, Keizersberg and Vlierbeek and the abbey of St. Geertrui
- M Museum for ancient as well as contemporary art
- The University Library, climb the bell tower and be rewarded with splendid views

Toerisme Leuven
Naamsestraat 3
B-3000 Leuven
+32(0)16/20 30 20
www.leuven.be

→ Leuven, town hall

EN STOEMELINGS

Curieuse Neus, En Stoemelings

Brussels has gained another neighbourhood brewery. Just take a peek through the window. With any luck, you will see the brewer at work. **TIP:** browse the daily open air antiques market held at Vossenplein (place du Jeu de Balle) and the indoor market selling organic produce just around the corner at Huidevettersstraat (rue des Tanneurs).

You are welcome to pop in every Tuesday to Saturday between the hours of 1100 and 1800.

Spiegelstraat 1/1 rue du Miroir, Brussels
+32(0)489/49 59 24
www.enstoemelings.be

GIRARDIN

Girardin

A lambic brewery was set up in 1845 in grounds owned by the aristocracy. In 1882 this farm-brewery was acquired by the Girardin family who, four generations down the line, are still managing the business. This brewery enjoys a unique location. It can be spotted from far away at the top of Lindenberg hill, surrounded by fields. The Girardin family cultivates its own grain for brewing.

The brewery is closed to visitors.

Lindenberg 10, Sint-Ulriks-Kapelle
+32(0)2/453 94 19

HAACHT

Adler, Export 8, Gildenbier, Keizer Karel, Mystic, Ommegang, Primus, Spéciale 1900, Star, Tongerlo, White by Mystic

The third largest brewery in Belgium, after AB Inbev and Alken-Maes, was established in the first half of the 19th century. A brewhall was added in 1989 and the former maltings are now used for storage. Eugène De Ro, the founder, launched a bottom-fermented beer in 1902. Ten years later, Haacht already ranked amongst the top brewers in Belgium despite its humble beginnings as a dairy in 1893. The lovely brewhall with elements of art nouveau, no longer in use, was built in the 1920s whereas the still operational brewhall was built in the 1930s. Haacht established a bottling plant in 1950 and, one year on, the brewery was acquired by son-in-law Alfred Van der Kelen. The fourth generation is now in charge. The brewery's flagship beer is Primus pils, named after Jan Primus, Duke of Brabant who was known for his love of beer. The unfiltered and unpasteurised Primus with its yeast clearly visible can only be sampled at Het Brouwershof, straight across from the brewery. Export 8 is a cold storage beer that, between 1925 and 1975, was very popular with the working classes. It often made an appearance at festivals and fun fairs. Spéciale 1900 is an amber beer that fits within the *spéciale belge* style. This brand was acquired from the Brussels-based Aerts brewery after a take-over by Haacht. The abbey beers of Tongerlo are brewed under licence. At Tongerlo, brewing activity can be traced all the way back to 1130. Tongerlo Prior is a complex beer, made with barley and wheat; it tastes zesty and fruity. A small yeast glass is placed on the side of every order.

Tours by prior arrangement for groups comprising 15 - 50. Your guided visit concludes with a beer tasting in Het Brouwershof.

Brouwerij Haacht,
Provinciesteenweg 28, Boortmeerbeek
+32(0)16/60 15 01 – visit@haacht.com
www.haacht.com

HANSSENS ARTISANAAL

Hanssens Artisanaal Oude Geuze, Oude Kriek, Oud Beitje

In 1896 the Mayor of Dworp, Bartholomé Hanssens, purchased an old dairy farm and converted it into a brewery which he named Sint-Antonius. He produced a brown table beer rather than lambic which was, after all, produced by many of his colleagues in the village. After the First World War Bartholomé decided to specialise in cutting wort purchased elsewhere. The brewery turned into a gueuzestekerij. Here you won't find large stainless steel fermentation tanks; instead, there is a small space with a dusty attic full of old barrels made of wood. When you enter the building you will see, next to the stairs leading to the fermentation loft, the largest wooden barrel owned by Hanssens. It was used for cutting the lambic and even provided a shelter for war refugees. Hanssens Artisanaal also produces Oud Beitje, a strawberry lambic primarily promoted as an aperitif. In addition to his artisan old gueuze and old kriek, the brewer produces two fruit preserves, one made with gueuze and one with kriek.

Authentic gueuzestekerij with vintage equipment under the roof of a farm owned by the fourth generation of the Hanssens family. Call them to arrange your visit.

Vroenenbosstraat 15, Dworp
+32(0)2/380 31 33

HERBERG (Den)

Den Herberg Amber, Blond, Bruin, Tarwe, Tripel

De Gouden Lantaarn, a former village hall in Buizingen near Halle, has been transformed into a craft brewery with its own, cycle-friendly, café. Often a venue for live music, this place is always bustling. The seats, the glow from the open fire, the wooden staircase... and the room on the first floor where magicians like to show off their skills. Bart Duvillé, the brewer, is also a jack-in-the-box: café manager, instrument builder, building contractor and, to top it all off, father to seven children.

A genuine café brewery where brewing takes place in the former village party hall. For night owls as well as early birds. Open Monday – Thursday and on Sundays from 1100 to 0100. On Fridays and Saturdays, from 1100 to 0300.

Octave De Kerckhove d'Exaerdestraat 16, Buizingen
+32(0)2/305 36 56 of +32(0)476/41 92 67
www.denherberg.be

HOEGAARDEN

Hoegaarden, Grand Cru, Rosée, Spéciale, Verboden Vrucht, Witbier

Strange but true: around 1726, Hoegaarden was home to as many as 36 breweries. Why so many? Simply because the brewers here had to cough up fewer taxes. The beer epoch commences around 1445 when the monks divided their time between prayer, worship, wine making and beer brewing. They came up with a recipe for a slightly sour white beer. As, in those days, the region formed part of the Netherlands, the monks were able to use exotic herbs and spices from the Dutch Indies and did not hesitate to use orange peel and coriander. However, the traditional white beer was wiped off the map after the pils revolution. The last brewery closed its doors in 1957. Enter... Pierre Celis. In 1965 this milkman decided to revive this beer style. He started brewing in his shed with one copper kettle. Celis then moved to the larger De Kluis building. Hoegaarden is now owned by AB Inbev. The white beer contains pure wheat and wheat malt. Two different original yeasts are used for the main fermentation and the re-fermentation. Aroma hops are also an ingredient but are barely discernible in the beer. 'Let it rest in the cellar for a month, it will be at its peak by then', the

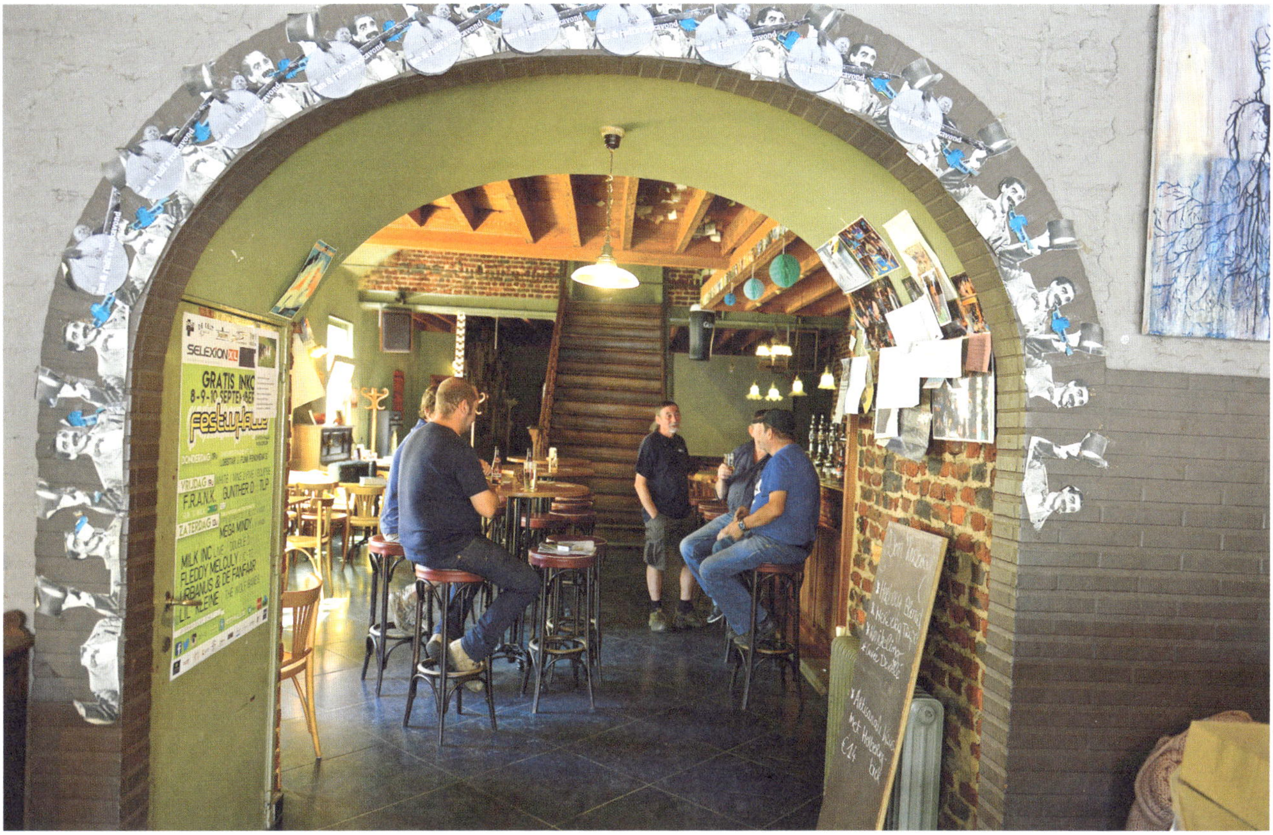
SELEXION XL
GRATIS INKO
8-9-10 SEPTE
DONDERDAG
VRIJDAG
F.R.A.N.K.
GUNTHER D
TLP
ZATERDAG
MEGA MINDY
MILK INC
FLEDDY MELCULY
URBANUS & DE FANFAAR
LIL' KLEINE

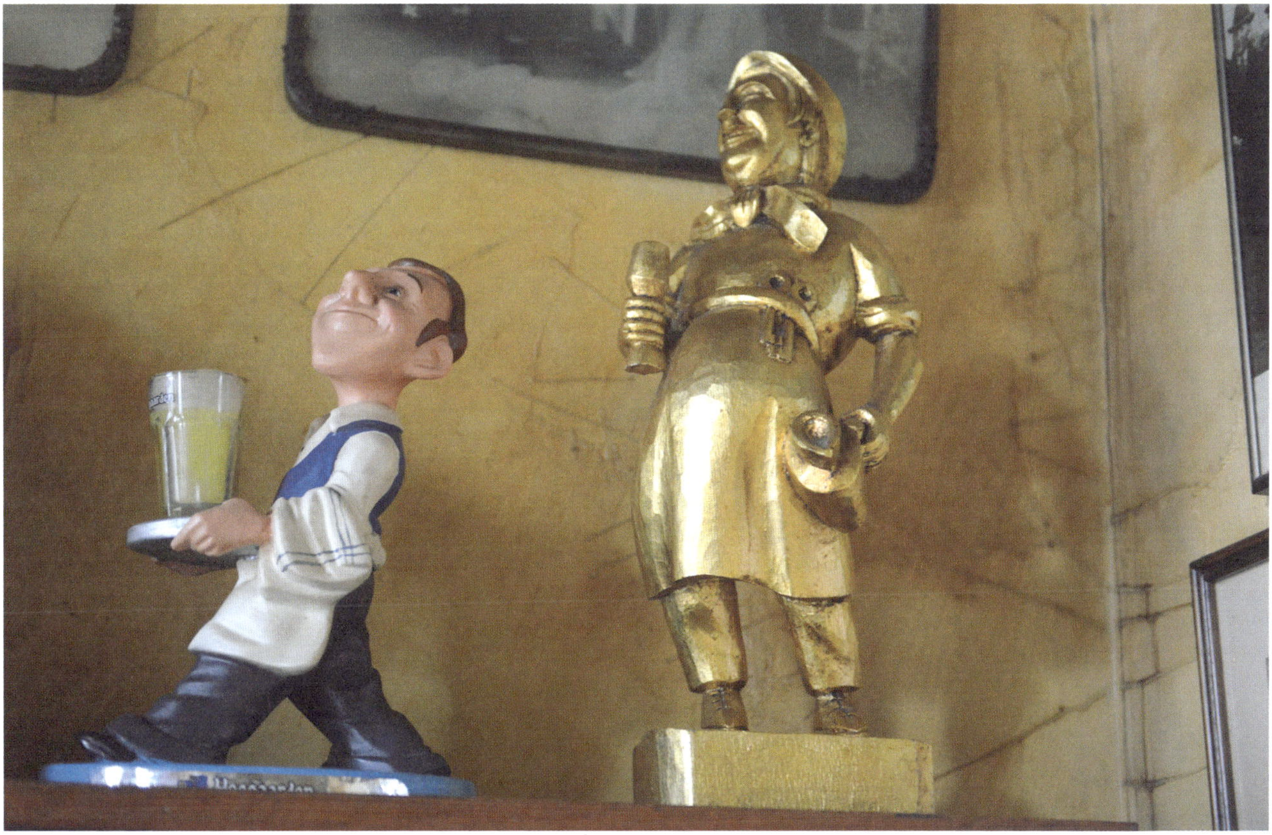

brewer advises. Malt, wheat, hop, coriander, dried orange peel and water still determine the taste. This 'witte van Hoegaarden' grew in popularity thanks to mouth-to-mouth advertising and the iconic beer mat campaign. The unfiltered beer with its natural look was an instant success amongst young people. In later years Pierre Celis was to launch the Celis White in the US. Tip: cycle along the Bieren- en Bietenroute (42.2 km).

Visit the birthplace of the world's best known white beer on a Wednesday or Thursday. The guided tour at 1300 is open to all. Group visits are held at 1030 and 1400 and require prior reservation. Discover the history, the ingredients, the brewing process and trivia you may or may not know.

Stoopkensstraat 24a, Hoegaarden
+32(0)16/76 78 43 – info@breweryvisits.com
www.breweryvisits.com

HOF TEN DORMAAL

Dormaal, Inferno, Kriek, Oak Aged Extra Strong Blond & Dark, Zure van Tildonk

The imposing farming estate of Dormaal is surrounded by fields. 'We grow our own barley and hops for brewing. Our energy is provided by rapeseed from our own fields. We are also cattle farmers and use the 'waste products' as fodder. And this closes the circle', explain farmer-brewer André Janssens and his sons Dries and Jef. Their endive beer is quite the odd one out: it is brewed partly with chicory root and partly with hops. Hof Ten Dormaal has made a name for itself with its barrel aged beers. All three of the Janssens are keen on following tradition and pairing it with innovation. This is why they like to think outside the box. They stage the annual Leuven Innovation Beer Festival and invite microbreweries to take part. Hof Ten Dormaal goes for 'experimenting with tradition'. Taste blond and dark beers matured on barrels previously used for sherry, calvados, whisky or port. Their range of Taste Lab beers veers even further away from the well-trodden paths with its use of unusual ingredients – wild fruits, blackthorn berries... - resulting in surprisingly different aromas and tastes. **TIP:** enjoy the beers at the Engelenburcht restaurant (www.engelenburchtmyresto.be) in Tildonk (Haacht).

The brewhall and its café are open every Saturday from 1400 to 1700. Guided tours are arranged on request.

Caubergstraat 2, Tildonk
+32(0)477/51 59 91
www.hoftendormaal.com

JANDRAIN-JANDRENOUILLE
(Brasserie de)

Archiduc, Big Mama, Djan d'Nivèle, IV Saison, V Cense, VI Wheat

The brewery is housed in an 18th century farmhouse, built in the traditional square style. The image of the 'IV' that towers over the hop fields on the label of the IV Saison was designed by well-known Brussels cartoonist François Schuiten. This 'IV' refers to the four basic components of the beer and also to the *saison*, a traditional farm beer from the area. The brewery also produces the amber-coloured V Cense. 'We make a completely artisan, unfiltered beer, using *dry hopping* and in-bottle re-fermentation', brewer Alexandre Dumont de Chassart assures us. This engineer likes balance. He does not aim to produce a niche beer but is after one with plenty of hop bitter that goes down easily. 'We want to create an excellent product with lots of common sense and character. You can make a great beer just with the basic ingredients, provided they are of good quality.' These beers stand out through their rich hop aromas. 'The hop lies at the foundation', Alexandre confirms. 'We want to taste what we put into our beers. A thirst-quenching beer with a great finish.' VI Wheat, a white beer, is a pure wheat beer without the addition of curaçao and coriander. The brewer is keen on using American aroma hops where appropriate, hence the touches of mango and lychee in the beer. 'I dream of well-hopped, quaffable beers brewed with Belgian know-how.' The taste of Belgian beer drinkers is too limited, he finds. They are too easily satisfied with an average thirstquencher. This brewer provides his own interpretation of traditional Belgian beer styles like saison or white beer by adding imported American aroma hops. His malt comes from locally grown barley. **TIP:** visit Hoegaarden, the birthplace of white beer.

Tours on request for groups of 10 and over.

> Rue de la Féculerie 34,
> Jandrain-Jandrenouille (Orp-Jauche)
> +32(0)19/51 42 98 of +32(0)475/71 45 35
> alexandre.dumont@skynet.be
> www.brasseriedejandrainjandrenouille.com

NAMUR

Things to see and do
- The Church of St. Gertrude with its bell tower and crypt
- the historic city centre
- the Musée Communal with its collections of archaeology, art and history
- the car museum with its American vintage cars
- La Dodaine city park

Tip: taste the savoury 'tarte al djote' with a regional beer on the side

Tourisme Nivelles
Rue de Saintes 48
B – 1400 Nivelles
+32(0)67/21 54 13
info@tourisme-nivelles.be
www.tourisme-nivelles.be

KROON (De)

Delvaux, Job, Superkroon

A warm welcome is guaranteed by Freddy and Filip Delvaux, beer fermentation experts. They established a brewery museum and a microbrewery on the site of a former brewery. You can taste the house beers in the tavern and enjoy its brasserie cuisine where beer takes a starring role. **TIP:** walk or cycle in this green oasis or visit Louvain.

Visit by prior arrangement. The tavern is open to anyone, not just visitors to the brewery.

Beekstraat 20, Neerijse
+32(0)16/43 94 72
info@brouwerijdekroon.be
www.brouwerijdekroon.be

LEFÈBVRE

Barbãr, Belgian fruit beers, Blanche de Bruxelles, Floreffe, Hopus, Newton, Saison 1900

The reputation of the Lefèbvre brewery dates from 1876. Several cafés opened their doors in the vicinity of the Quenast quarries to allow the stonemasons to quench their thirst. At the time, the quarries employed a workforce of 3500. Jules Lefèbvre, a gamekeeper, farmer, innkeeper, malt worker and stand-up comedian to boot, decided to set up a new brewery that would supply the inns with a (light) beer. In 1975 the torch was passed to Philippe who represented the fifth generation of this brewing dynasty. His son Paul-Emile is the sixth-generation scion to manage the brewery. Under licence, Lefèbvre is now brewing the Bonne Espérance and Floreffe abbey beers as well as Blanche de Bruxelles white beer, Barbãr honey beer and Newton apple beer.

Blanche de Bruxelles is the brewery's flagship beer and accounts for just under half of the volume produced. The fruit beer is also based on this 'witte'. In the 1960s Lefèbvre focused on producing heavier specialty beers such as Porph-Ale, a *spéciale belge*. The well-hopped Hopus is not complete without a small yeast glass. You can enjoy the beer with the yeast at the bottom to keep it till last, blend it in, or enjoy the beer and the yeast separately. The choice is yours.

The brewery is closed to the public. A 'beer house' dedicated to Lefèbvre products is located at the picturesque site of Kleine Molen van Arenberg in nearby Rebecq. Taste the Lefèbvre beers in the tavern right next to the beer museum.

Chemin du Croly 54, Quenast
+32(0)67/67 07 66
www.brasserielefebvre.be
Petit Moulin d'Arenberg,
rue Docteur Colson 8, Rebecq
+32(0)67/67 07 66 – +32(0)67 63 82 32

LINDEMANS

BlossomGueuze, Oude Gueuze & Oude Kriek Cuvée René, Kriek, Gueuze, Faro, Pecheresse, Framboise, Cassis & Apple Lindemans, SpontanBasil

Seven generations ago, in 1809, the Lindemans family owned and managed a farm: Hof ter Kwade Wegen in Vlezenbeek near Brussels. During the long and dark winter months, a small lambic brewery operated at the farm keeping everyone in work. Brewing gradually gained in importance to the detriment of agriculture. The main activity in those days was selling wort and lambic to farmers and cafés. The café owners purchased the wort, allowed it to fully ferment and used this lambic to produce gueuze, faro and kriek. These 'gueuzestekerijen' would become Lindemans customers. Conversely, Lindemans is now a supplier of wort to De Cam, 3 Fonteinen and Hanssens. The brewery focused on fruity and sweet fruit beers and saw its international sales rise. Old gueuze was no longer made as all of the lambic was required for the fruit beers. However, in response to a request from the USA, the Oude Geuze was once more included in the range from 1994 onwards under the new name of Cuvée René. 1978 saw the relaunch of Faro, a drink enjoyed by the people in Breughelian times, which had pretty much disappeared from the market. In recent years this lambic brewery has introduced its ground-breaking *botanicals*, lambic beers enriched with basil, elderflower and other ingredients. There is also a gin distilled on the basis of Lindemans lambics. **TIP:** visit Gaasbeek Castle or the Coloma Rose Garden. Taste the beers in the Klosken farm inn (www.klosken.com).

Guided tours Monday to Friday between 0800 and 1800. Maximum of 25 participants per guide. Booking necessary.

Lenniksebaan 297, Vlezenbeek
(Sint-Pieters-Leeuw)
+32(0)2/569 03 90
info@lindemans.be – www.lindemans.be

LOTERBOL

Loterbol, Tuverbol

'Loterbol' is the nickname given by the citizens of Mechelen to the 'madmen' of Diest. A 'loterbol' is a ball that keeps rolling around for lack of a centre. Marc Beirens now produces a beer with the same name, giving fresh impetus to the rich Diest wheat beer and white beer tradition. 'Our Tuverbol started off as an experiment', he tells us. 'When I was brewing the blond Loterbol, I kept my first few brews on the side. The beer was bottled after its spontaneous fermentation but I did not sell a lot of it. I then got the idea of blending the strong blond Loterbol with a young lambic.' Beirens knocked on the door at 3 Fonteinen in Beersel. And so, the young lambic made at 3 Fonteinen was exposed to the charms of a Diest blonde. A successful union between Hageland and the Senne valley. This brewer goes for 'healthily bitter beers with a real beer taste'. **TIP:** visit the historic city of Diest and its beguinage.

Every first Saturday of the month this brewery, located in a renovated 18th century building, opens its doors from 1600 to midnight. Guided tours are available.

Michel Theysstraat 58a, Diest
+32(0)13/77 10 07 – loterbol@skynet.be
www.loterbol.be

MORT SUBITE

Mort Subite Kriek Lambic (Tradition), (Oude) Gueuze Lambic, Oude Kriek Lambic, Witte Lambic

This brewery was established at the end of the 17th century by Joris Van der Hasselt and, later on, by the De Keersmaeker family to whom Joris was related. The family would dedicate itself to the production of gueuze which they named Mort Subite. 'Mort Subite', or sudden death, refers to a dice game. When work called and the game had to end, the players were entitled to one last throw, the 'mort subite'. The loser was declared 'dead'. This lambic brewery uses the very latest technology to produce gueuze and kriek in the artisan way. 'You learn how to brew lambic by doing it', comments Bruno Reinders, the brewer. 'There is much you have to take into account: the effect of nature and of the seasons, different degrees of fermentation and temperature and all the while, you have to deliver a consistent product. Lambic brewers cannot afford to stand still. We are also using the advantages of modern technology. Just think of temperature control, unheard of in the olden days. This is how we manage to deliver a product with a consistent quality.' The only contact with oxygen is to start up the fermentation. Afterwards, the entire process takes place in closed tanks to protect the beer from harmful micro-organisms. 'We limit negative outside influences,' Bruno assures us. 'This is why we don't use an open cooling basin. The fermentation tanks contain air that is replete with wild yeasts and we also inject further air from time to time to fire up the fermentation.' **TIP:** take a walk along the Dertien Bunderswandelpad (10.5 km) that runs alongside the brewery.

Lambic brewery with lovely old brewhall and foeder chamber. Visit by prior arrangement. Guided tours only on weekdays for groups of between 10 and 50.

Reservation through
vzw Toerisme Brabantse Kouters
+32(0)2/270 99 30
www.brabantsekouters.be
Lierput 1, Kobbegem (Asse)
+32(0)2/454 11 11
infomortsubite@alken-maes.com
www.mort-subite.be

NIEUWHUYS

Alpaïde, Cuvée van de Generaal, Huardis, Rosdel

A man from Antwerp and a woman from Poperinge met in South Africa... and opened their Nieuwhuys café in the oldest (17th century) building in Hoegaarden that was both an inn and the town hall in a former life. They started brewing here in 2005. Jan and Mieke now have a separate brewery a few doors on. Their dark tripel has built quite a reputation for itself. Alpaïde is named after the Countess who ruled Hoegaarden in the Middle Ages. At the end of the 10th century she founded a chapter of canons and gave it the name of Huardis. Rosdel is named after a nature reserve in the area. 'Our craft beers are brewed locally in a village with a strong beer history,' Mieke tells us. 'We do everything ourselves here. We are very flexible as we operate on a small scale.' Ambitions are on a larger scale, however. Nieuwhuys is also offering house-distilled Dutch gin, liqueur and whisky.

The brewery is closed to the public but you can visit the café where the brewery was established originally. Open Thursday – Saturday from 1700 and from 1130 on a Sunday.

> Ernest Ourystraat 2
> +32(0)16/81 71 64
> jan@nieuwhuys.be
> www.nieuwhuys.be

OUD BEERSEL

Bersalis, Bzart lambiek & kriekenlambiek, Oud Beersel Oude Geuze, Oude Kriek & Framboise

Since 2005, Gueze has once again been 'cut' at Oude Beersel. Gueuzesteker Gert Christiaens: 'Besides Oude Geuze and Oude Kriek we also offer Bersalis Tripel, a blond top-fermented beer, and Bersalis Kadet, a top-fermented beer high in taste but low in alcohol. The success of these two beers has given me the opportunity to invest in lambic and old gueuze.' Oud Beersel is regarded as the bitterest lambic and gueuze thanks to the striking but light touches of hop. 'I buy in my lambic from Boon. They brew it based on my recipe. Spending far more time on quality control results in a lambic that is more tender, pleasant and accessible. The recipe has remained unchanged. This is a traditional lambic with plenty of taste and without acetic acid.' **TIP:** visit Beersel Castle and visitors' centre De Lambiek in Alsemberg.

A guide will be at the brewery every first and third Saturday of the month at 1130 and 1230. Reservations are required for group visits.

> Laarheidestraat 230, Beersel
> +32(0)486/69 36 29
> visit@degeuzenvanoudbeersel.be
> www.degeuzenvanoudbeersel.be

PALM BELGIAN CRAFT BREWERS/DE HOORN

Arthur's Legacy, Bruges Tripel, Estaminet, Cornet, Dobbel Palm, Palm, Palm Hop Select, Palm Royale, Palm Sauvin, SteenBruges

The history of Palm Belgian Craft Breweries commences in 1686 when Anna Cornet set up the De Hoorn village brewery opposite the church in Steenhuffel. The brewing trade carried on for generations. In 1975 the De Hoorn name was replaced by Palm. The brewery's eponymous flagship beer is an amber-coloured *spéciale belge* created at the start of the 20th century. In 1904 the Belgian brewery schools organised a contest with the aim of improving Belgian beer. The mission: to brew a stronger beer. The *spéciale belge* Palm stems from this tradition. 'Up to the 1950s the hop fields there extended all the way Asse and Aalst. Now, hops are few and far between', Paul Temmerman, a hop grower, tells us. Paul helped Palm establish their own hop field. This area is meant to be a support to local growers. The reign of sweet beers is losing its lustre and brewers are re-discovering hop. Hop is to beer what *cépage* is for wine. There is a vast range of bitter hops and aromatic varieties, from citric and fruity to floral, green or zesty, hoppy or noble. Palm opted for the popular Hallertau Mittelfrüh variety with its very delicate hoppy aroma. The brewer used it for his Palm Hop Select and liked its aromas so much that he added hop three times over: at the start and the end of the boiling process and in *dry hopping* towards the end of main fermentation. Otherwise, Palm Hop Select contains the same malts and yeast as the classic Palm. This extra hopped beer digests easily, goes down well and produces a robust head. **TIP:** use the cycling node network to follow the Brouwersroute (33, 65 or 100 km). It will take you past a range of breweries: Affligem, Bosteels, De Block, Duvel Moortgat, Malheur, Mort Subite and Palm Belgian Craft Brewers. Info: www.leireken.be

The brewery boasts a long tradition of producing top-fermented beers. The new De Hoorn microbrewery, set up on the brewery's site, is suitable for the production of smaller volumes. This is where the brewmasters are experimenting with the new Arthur's Legacy beers with their dominant taste of herbs and spices, fruit, wood or hops. Make an appointment and you will tour the brewery and microbrewery in the company of a professional guide. The tour starts in the visitors' centre, De Oude Bottelarij. Your first stop is the brewhall followed by the herb room, the fermentation chambers, the bottling plant and the distribution hall. Needless to say, your visit concludes with a tasting session. Guided tours are available to groups of 15-50 participants. There is also an opportunity to look around the stud farm for Brabant draught horses located in the grounds of Diepensteyn Castle.

Steenhuffeldorp 3, Steenhuffel (Londerzeel)
+32(0)52/31 74 14
www.palmbreweries.com

SCHUUR (De)

Meneer, Nikolaas

Jan Symons took a look around Hoegaarden and was instantly bitten by the brewing bug. Jan and his brother Bert knuckled down to work with hops, malt, candi sugar and wheat. Ever since 1994 the brothers have been brewing unfiltered, top-fermented beers that re-ferment in the bottle.

Visit by prior arrangement. Taste the beers in In den Hof in Linden café.

Wolvendreef 30, Linden
+32(0)16/62 13 58 of +32(0)485/37 61 35
www.brouwerijdeschuur.info

SENNE (Brasserie de la)

Brussels Calling, Crianza, Equinox, Jambe-de-Bois, Saison de la Senne, Schieve Tabarnak, Stouterik, Taras Boulba, Zinnebir, Zwarte Piet

In 2003 Bernard Leboucq started up the Sint-Pietersbrouwerij on the site of the former Moriau lambic brewery. At the time, he brewed his Zinnebir in milk churns. In 2005 Bernard Leboucq and Yvan De Baets happened to cross paths at the Zinnekeparade. They 'clicked' and decided to set up Brasserie de la Senne in partnership. After a three-year search they found a suitable space within an old industrial bakery right next to Oud-Molenbeek cemetery. Seeking finance and renovating the building took another year. Finally, on 22 December 2010 the first edition of Brussels Calling hit the market: a festive beer for Christmas and the New Year with a recipe that is tweaked every year. De Zennebrouwers have been applauded for their Zinnebir and Taras Boulba with their distinctive maltiness, hop bitterness and fruity yeast. The partners don't like to plan too far ahead or follow a laid-out path. 'We produce character beers that we like to drink ourselves. We are quite keen on sour beers, like the lambic beers from Cantillon, or bitter beers like the ones we make ourselves. Just like in the olden days, when sweet beers simply did not exist. We only work with water, malt, hop and yeast. And above all, we like to brew lighter beers with plenty of taste.' The brewers have experimented with mixed fermentation for a Flemish old brown and a saison 'in the style of the 19th century'. Both of these beers were left to mature in recycled wine casks. **TIP:** taste these beers with a meal in Les Brigittines restaurant (www.lesbrigittines.com) in the heart of Brussels.

Visit by prior arrangement for groups of 15 and over. The brewery is planning to move to a new, more spacious location close to Tour & Taxis on the Brussels canals.

Steenweg op Ghent 565, Brussels
+32(0)2/465 07 51 – info@brasseriedelasenne.be
www.brasseriedelasenne.be

TILQUIN
(Gueuzerie)

Oude Gueuze Tilquin, Oude Quetsche Tilquin, Gueuze Tilquin on tap

Pierre Tilquin trained as a gueuzesteker with 3 Fonteinen and Cantillon. Nowadays he works with lambic made by Girardin, Lindemans, Boon and Cantillon. Pierre strives to produce rounded beers in which you can taste the character of each different lambic. He is a born scientist and leaves nothing to chance. The barrels are cleaned at temperatures of 30 °C, 60 °C and 80 °C. Pierre wants to be in control of the entire process from start to finish, including the bottling. His gueuze contains a minimum of 10 per cent lambic from each brewery he works with. He adds liquid sugar to kick-start the fermentation. The beer then spends six months in the warm chamber (18 °C). The gueuze he sells is on average 2.5 years old. Pierre Tilquin is opposed to the myths that have now formed around gueuze. 'It is an accessible beer', he finds. 'I provide the best possible conditions for the lambic to mature.'

Visits by prior arrangement for groups with a minimum of 10 participants from Monday to Saturday. The brewery is open to visitors every Saturday between 1030 and 1300 when the brewery shop is open.

Chaussée Maïeur Habils 110, Bierges – +32(0)472/91 82 91 – info@gueuzerietilquin.be – www.gueuzerietilquin.be

TIMMERMANS

Timmermans Blanche Lambicus, Faro Lambicus, Framboise Lambicus, Kriek Retro Lambicus, Oude Gueuze Lambicus, Oude Kriek Lambicus, Pêche Lambicus, Pumpkin Lambicus, Strawberry Lambicus

Jacobus Walravens produced his first lambic brew in 1702. We are now eight generations down the line. In 1993 the brewery was incorporated into Anthony Martin' "The Finest Drinks Company". At Timmermans' you can enjoy a lambic, gueuze or faro as well as a fruit beer with natural aromas of kriek, peach and raspberry, amongst others. The brewhall of this active historic brewery contains grain silos, grain mills, a 'meeltremel' (used to store the malt and wheat before mashing), a warm water kettle, a mashing basin, a filtration basin and a boiling kettle. Lambic matures in oak barrels in the foeder halls. Beer architect Willem Van Herreweghen took the Timmermans lambic beers back to their roots. Lambiek is a pale, amber-coloured, spontaneously fermented beer with an ABV of 4.5 to 6° made with barley, wheat and hop. The wort is boiled for four to five hours, far longer than is required for a pils beer. The mixture, consisting of extracts of barley malt and wheat, is left to cool down overnight in the koelschip, or cooling basin. During this time spent in the open air the wild

yeasts permeate the wort. The main ones are *Brettanomyces bruxellensis* and *Brettanomyces lambicus*. Both are typical for the valley of the Senne and bring about the specific taste. Once cooled down, the beer will spend at least six months fermenting in oak barrels. Some of it will be left to mature for over three years. Lambic is a flat beer, low in carbon dioxide, with a sourish taste. Pure lambic is not unlike a cider or *fino sherry* and comes with a long finish. **TIP:** visit Huis Mostinckx and Dilbeek hop museum.

In the oldest lambic brewery in the world that is still in operation, the original infrastructure is used to this day. Explore three hundred years of Belgian brewing history in the brewery museum. The brewery is open daily, including weekends, by pre-arrangement only. Guided tours are available. Tip: a signposted Breughel walk passes the brewery. There are also bike routes. Info: www.dilbeek.be

Kerkstraat 11, Itterbeek (Dilbeek)
+32(0)2/569 03 57
www.anthonymartin.be/timmermans

TRIEST (Den)

Bruut'n Triest, De Neus, Den Triest Blond, Dubbel, Kesse, Kriek & Tripel, Greenhopping

'Triest' means 'farmland'. Walkers or cyclists who are making a trip along the Willebroek Canal or follow one of the four bike trails or three walking routes in the area of Kapelle-op-den-Bos will pass the Den Triest brewery. Brouwer Marc Struyf collects beer labels. He has now collected over 50,000 of them, which makes Marc's collection the largest of its kind in Belgium. As befits a label collector, he carefully attaches each label to his own bottles by hand. Marc is an avid collector and the walls of his little café at the back of the garden, right opposite his home brewery, prove the point. All of the vintage enamel signs covering the walls; each plate, bottle or glass tells its own brewery story. Marc likes to brew with home-grown hops wherever possible. De Neus, a triple, refers to the nickname given to the citizens of Kapelle. They are said to look down on the rest of the world with their nose, or 'neus', firmly stuck in the air. Marc is well connected with the microbrewing community and feels a

particular affinity with the USA. For his beers, he uses European hops as well as aromatic varieties from New Zealand and the USA. **TIP:** pay a visit to the Weldebrouck brewery (Antwerp region).

On the first Sunday of every month, the brewery and its café are open between 1300 and 1800. Group visits (minimum of 15) welcome by prior arrangement.

>Triestraat 24, Kapelle-op-den-Bos
>+32(0)475/74 38 05
>info@dentriest.be
>www.dentriest.be

TROCH (De)

Chapeau Abricot, Banana, Exotic, Faro, Fraise, Framboise, Gueuze, Kriek, Lemon, Peche, Cuvée Oude Gueuze

This small but beautiful brewery was built in the tower style in a self-contained farmhouse in the heart of Wambeek. De Troch is the only lambic brewery to pair traditional gueuze with the exotic tastes of mango and banana, strawberry, lemon, peach and lime. Its history goes back to 1796. To this day, the copper brewing kettles are heated by coal on an open fire. The process commences when the grain (30 per cent ground wheat and 70 percent ground barley) is mixed with water and boiled for several minutes. The resulting wort is transferred to a boiling kettle and blended with aged hop. This type of hop does not have the bitter taste provided by fresh hops but it has the same beer-preserving qualities. The wort will boil for around 3.5 hours. The brew is then pumped across to the koelschip or cooling basin, which is exposed to the open air. This is where the spontaneous fermentation happens. The wort will take the entire night to cool down and during that time, the *Brettanomyces bruxellensis* and *Brettanomyces lambicus* yeasts start permeating the liquid. The following morning the wort will be transferred to oak barrels where it starts the slow maturation process. The sugars are converted into alcohol. In the meantime, the wild yeasts are doing their work, providing the complex patterns of taste and aroma typical of lambic. The beer matures for several months or even years.

Visit this brewery by pre-arrangement, individually or as part of a group.

>Langestraat 20, Wambeek (Ternat)
>+32(0)2/582 10 27
>info@detroch.be
>www.detroch.be

TUBIZE (Brasserie de)

Abbaye de Boneffe, Betchard

Jean Rodriguez of In 't Spinnekopke, an 'estaminet' in Brussels, had been dreaming of setting up his own artisan brewery for a long time. In 2009 he established Brasserie de Tubize with a beer restaurant next door on the site of a factory that used to produce synthetic silk on the banks of the river Senne. Jean Rodriguez aims to produce light beers. 'Brewing is like cooking. You play around with the yeast mixture and the varieties of hops and malt.' Betchard, the local character who has given his name to this beer, was a town crier who used to announce the news to the villagers in full voice. He was considered a braggart and a bad payer, 'especially when he had been drinking'. Betchard is now Tubize's town beer. 'I like to keep things small', Jean reveals. 'I am brewing for fun. My brewery should not turn into a factory.' **TIP:** discover hundreds of Belgian beers and taste Belgian (beer) cuisine at In 't Spinnekopke in the heart of Brussels.

A visit with tasting is available by pre-arrangement.

Rue de la Filature 2, Tubize
+32(0)475/24 63 37
brasseriedetubize@gmail.com
In 't Spinnekopke, Bloementuinplein 1, Brussels
+32(0)2/511 86 95 – www.spinnekopke.be

VAN CAMPENHOUT

Wit Lov

Kris Smedts and Mieke Nijs are brewing artisan beers on the site of the former De Biertoren brewery. The old malt works has been converted into a party hall. The name of the beer, Wit Lov, is a nod to the 'white gold' that is prolific in this region. However, 'witloof' or endives do not feature on the list of ingredients. Tip: a great walking and cycling destination halfway between Mechelen and Louvain (Leuven); can be combined with a visit to Planckendael Zoo. A 51km cycle track leads to Rotselaar and passes the Haacht and Hof Ten Dormaal breweries.

Open to visitors every first Sunday of the month at 1500 hours. Taste the beers and brasserie cuisine in the Labo Café with its regular live music performances. **TIP:** the house pizza is made with beer yeast.

Brouwerijstraat 23F, Kampenhout
+32(0)16/22 64 66
info@brouwerijvancampenhout.be
www.brouwerijvancampenhout.be

VILLERS-LA-VILLE (Abbaye de)

Abbaye de Villers Blond & Tripel

Amongst the ruins of the abbey of Villers-la-Ville you come across what is left of a brewery. It is thought that there was a brewery in the grounds from the 13th century but its precise location is unknown. Nevertheless, it has been established that brewing took place in the former guest house between the 16th and the 18th century. At the time, three types of beer were produced: a strong beer for the monks, a lighter beer for guests and a very light beer for domestic staff and labourers. It is far from a coincidence that brewing was done in the abbey. After all, the monks had the experience required, the knowledge, the funds and the manpower. Also, all the ingredients could be procured from within the abbey grounds and power was produced by a water mill. A brand new microbrewery has now been established in the former laundry room right next to the water mill. The latest generation of organic abbey beers is based on a contemporary recipe. **TIP:** visit the imposing ruins of the abbey and its gardens to get an impression of the large-scale activities in which the abbeys were involved in the era prior to the French Revolution (1789–1794).

You can visit the brewery by prior arrangement.

Rue de l'Abbaye 55, Villers-la-Ville – +32(0)71/88 09 80 – info@villers.be – www.villers.be

VISSENAKEN

De Nacht, Fasso, Meetsel, Himelein

The beers made by Rudy Scheys are steeped in history. Himelein is a reference to an Irish monk who travelled across the sea to convert the local population. Rudy reveals that he discovered the world of beer after a course of... wine tasting. Straight away he was sold on the 'world of tastes combined with fruit, herbs and spices and sugar.' **TIP:** visit the 'sugar town' of Tienen.

Pre-arrange your visit for groups of between 7 and 12 participants.

Metselstraat 74, Vissenaken (Tienen)
+32(0)16/82 13 77
brouwerij.vissenaken@skynet.be
www.brouwerijvissenaken.net

↑ Villers-la-Ville, ruins of the abbey

VLIER (De)

Amber 69, Brut, Carroussel, De Vlier-range, Ferme Framboos, Gulden Delle, Holsbeekse Lentetripel, Onbekende Soldaat, Smokin' Elder, Xmas Spicy, Winter Stout

Marc Andries is consumed by beer. This bio-engineer has spent many years working in breweries and, in his basement, brewed what was for him 'the ideal beer'. Brouwerij De Vlier was founded in 2008. Its name is based on the village of Vlierbeek, where the brewery started off. 'Our aperitif beers (Gulden Delle, Ferme Framboos and Brut) are our response to sparkling wines, cava and champagne - demi-sec, rosé and brut', Marc Andries laughs. Taste the traces of lactic acid in sparkling celebration beers. Balanced, very drinkable and yet not too predictable. **TIP:** visit Louvain (Leuven), Vlierbeek abbey, Horst Castle, the Kessel-Lo recreation area, walk or cycle in the lovely Hageland landscape.

The tasting room is open every Saturday between 1600 and 2000. A guided tour takes place at 1500. Groups comprising up to 12 participants are welcome by prior arrangement.

Leuvensebaan 219, Holsbeek
+32(0)473/83 94 63
info@brouwerijdevlier.com
www.brouwerij-devlier.com

WATERLOO
(Brasserie de)

Waterloo, Récolte, Tripel Blond, Strong Oak, Cuvée Impériale, Strong Kriek

The Ferme de Mont Saint-Jean formed the backdrop to a major event in history. The farm was converted into a field hospital during the famous Battle of Waterloo. This imposing square farm is now owned by Anthony Martin's Finest Drinks. The farmhouse itself with its barns, stables, pigsty, oven, well and chapel have been preserved. A brand new microbrewery was recently set up in one of the wings of the building. The farm does not only house the brewery. The site also comprises a restaurant, L'Orangerie du Prince, and a museum about the Battle of Waterloo. **TIP:** visit the battlefield and the war monuments in Waterloo and the nearby City of Nivelles.

Guided tours by prior arrangement.

Chaussée de Charleroi 591, Waterloo
+32(0)2 38 50 103 – www.waterloo-beer.com

WATERLOO

Things to see and do
- the Butte du Lion (Lion's Mound) of Waterloo for its views of the battlefield
- the 1815 memorial with its panoramic painting that takes you right into the heart of the battle
- the Wellington Museum
- Napoleon's last headquarters
- the historic monuments and farms involved in the Battle of Waterloo
- Domaine Solvay at La Hulpe

Tourisme Waterloo
Chaussée de Bruxelles 218, B-1410 Waterloo
+32(0)2/352 09 10
www.waterloo-tourisme.com

THINGS TO SEE AND DO

AARSCHOTSE BRUINE

Good news for beer lovers: the 'Aarschotse Bruine' is once again flowing from the taps in the Municipal Museum. This is a slightly sour beer. In the beer experience centre you can smell and feel the hops and malt and follow the entire brewing process on video.

Toerisme Aarschot
+32(0)16/56 97 05
toerisme@aarschot.be

GRIMBERGEN ABBEY

Grimbergen

Grimbergen is the oldest inhabited Norbertine abbey in Belgium. The abbey was founded between 1126 and 1128. In 1816 this monastery was razed to the ground but its church, vicarage, farmhouse and the ancient entry gate were spared. The interior of the Basilica of St. Servaes (17th century) makes great use of the light coming in through its windows to display its particularly rich decoration. Organ concerts are staged from time to time. Grimbergen has risen from the ashes and this is why the brothers chose the phoenix as their emblem: the symbol of eternal rebirth. Even though no beer has been brewed at the abbey ever since the French Revolution, the Grimbergen abbey beer has survived. Alken-Maes has now taken over production and distribution. An abbey beer museum has been established in the old gatehouse of the abbey.

Abdij, Kerkplein 1, Grimbergen
+32(0)2/272 40 77
www.abdijgrimbergen.be

The basilica is open every day from 0700 to 1900. The abbey is not open to the public. Guided tours are available.

Abdijbiermuseum, Abdijstraat 2, Grimbergen.
Guided tours available.
Contact: Tourist Office, Prinsenstraat 22, Grimbergen
+32(0)2/270 99 30
www.abdijgrimbergen.be

Fenikshof, Abdijstraat 20
+32(0)2/306 39 56
www.hetfenikshof.be
The Fenikshof Brasserie is located in the grounds of Grimbergen abbey.

(DE LAMBIEK) VISITORS' CENTRE

This visitors' centre focuses on experience and discovery. Visitors are immersed in the tastes, aromas, sounds and textures of lambic beer. This visitors' centre is a highly recommended starting point if you want to get to know several lambic breweries as well as the Pajottenland area and the valley of the Senne. Not far away you will find Beersel Castle, the Herisem Mill as well as various lambic breweries and 'gueuzestekerijen', workshops where different gueuzes are blended. There is a brewery walk that departs from De Lambiek and guides you past several breweries. On the way you encounter information displays with plenty of explanation as well as vintage equipment used in lambic breweries, including a barrel cleaner that now takes pride of place at a roundabout in the village of Lot. Pick up a brochure for a detailed description of this walk.

Gemeenveldstraat 1, Alsemberg
+32(0)2/359 16 36
toerisme@beersel.be
www.beersel.be

Waterloo, the Lion

THE MUSEUM OF THE BELGIAN BREWERS

This museum comprises three parts: an 18th century brewery (transported from Hoegaarden), a high-tech modern brewery and an inn located in the vaulted basement. A brief but thorough overview of the ingredients of beer teaches you all you need to know. The brewing process is explained through video and computer screens allow you to find out about export statistics of breweries and malt works, explore all the varieties of beer and discover the secrets of the different ways of fermentation. Only a few steps separate you from a gleaming, but rather chilly modern brewery and a 'romantic', albeit quite aged and dusty vintage brewery from the 18th century. An amazingly vast collection of brewing equipment (used by brewers as well as coopers) provides a feast for the eyes. It's hard to imagine that beer was ever made in these brewing kettles and yeast basins. Luckily, St. Arnold is still keeping a watchful eye. At the end of your visit you can enjoy a good glass of beer at the inn located in the vaulted basement and admire a splendid collection of beer jugs and vintage café paraphernalia. Every week the beer served here comes from a different brewer and the identity of the beer and its brewer is a well-kept secret.

Open daily between 1000 and 1700 (from 01/12 to 31/03 the museum opens at 1200 on Saturday and Sunday).

Grote Markt 10, Brussels
+32(0)2/511 49 87
www.belgianbrewers.be

SCHAARBEEKS BIERMUSEUM (SCHAARBEEK BEER MUSEUM)

Beer connoisseurs don't need to be told that the best krieken lambic is made with Schaarbeek krieken cherries. Here, we are talking about a particular cherry variety rather than fruit grown in this Brussels municipality. The Schaarbeek Bier Museum is located in a slightly forlorn, quite peculiar location at Louis Bertrandlaan, which takes us back in a flash to the belle époque of the early 1920s. The museum has found a home in a school workshop. Where pupils were once taught different skills and trades, you can now receive a brief introduction into the history of Belgian beer. The brewing process is explained with varying pieces of brewery equipment close to hand. Much attention is paid to the traditional beer styles of Belgium, in particular lambic, faro, gueuze and kriek. All of these are typical for Brussels and the surrounding area. The museum walls are covered in vintage enamel signs, advertising beers that are often no longer around. Well over 1500 Belgian beer bottles and glasses are on display, categorised alphabetically by brewery. The collection comprises current breweries and brands as well as those who are no longer on the market. Admire the range on display and find out that Duvel used to be served in a flute glass. A tiny café complete with all of its fixtures and fittings takes you back to the years between 1900 and 1930. Tip: if you are thirsty for more, take a left turn when you leave the museum. On the corner of the street you will find specialty beer shop and café Le Barboteur.

The museum is open every Wednesday and Saturday between 1400 and 1800. Group visits by appointment.

Schaarbeeks Biermuseum,
Louis Bertrandlaan 33, Brussels
+32(0)2/241 56 27
http://users.skynet.be/museedelabiere/html/visite.html

TOERISME BRUSSELS
Koningstraat 2
B-1000 Brussels
+32(0)2/513 89 40
www.visitbrussels.be

TOERISME VLAAMS-BRABANT
Provincieplein 1,
B-3000 Louvain (Leuven)
+32(0)16/26 76 20
toerisme@vlaamsbrabant.be
www.toerismevlaamsbrabant.be

TOERISME PAJOTTENLAND & ZENNEVALLEI
Grote Markt 1, bus 1
B-1500 Halle
+32(0)2/356 42 59
info@toerisme-pajottenland.be
www.toerisme-pajottenland.be

TOURISME BRABANT WALLON
Parc des Collines
Bâtiment Afchimède
Avenue Einstein 2
B-1300 Wavre
+32(0)10/23 63 31
info@destinationbw.be
www.destinationbw.be

↑ Leuven, town hall

AALST
GHENT
GERAARDSBERGEN
NINOVE
OUDENAARDE
SINT-NIKLAAS

BOELENS

Bieken, Dubbel Klok, Tripel Klok, Santa Bee, Waase Wolf, Waaslander

At the request of the City of Antwerp, the Boelens brewery came up with a honey beer proprietary to Antwerp. Bee hives were dispersed around Antwerp city centre. The brewer received a donation of 40 kilos of honey from the city beekeeper, enabling him to brew the first Antwerp honey beer. The honey and the wort were boiled together to reduce the sweet taste but retain the mild flavour of honey. **TIPS:** there is a village church close by with beautiful wood carvings, a park just made for walking and numerous village cafés offering Klok beer on tap.

Visit by prior arrangement for groups of between 12 and 50.

Kerkstraat 7, Belsele (Sint-Niklaas)
+32(0)3/772 32 00
info@brouwerijboelens.be
www.brouwerijboelens.be

BOSTEELS

DeuS Brut des Flandres, Pauwels Kwak, Tripel Karmeliet

The unique stirrup glass proprietary to the Kwak beer is better known than the brewery itself. Drinking a metre of beer? No, this is not a joke. Order a Kwak and you will see for yourself. Kwak is a fruity amber beer with a malty aroma and, in the mouth, hints of herbs and spices, caramelised banana as well as bitter. The most striking aspect of this beer is the glass. Legend has it that once upon a time a brewer called Paul Kwak lived in Dendermonde. Paul owned an inn where mail coaches made regular stops. However, the coach drivers were not allowed to leave their horse-drawn vehicles alone, which meant that they were unable to enjoy a Kwak. Paul came up with an ingenious solution. He developed a glass with the proportions that we know to this day and that could be fixed easily to the walls of the coach. Problem solved. The Kwak glass is no longer affixed to the coach but the beer is still served in its own special glass and stand. Brouwerij Bosteels is over two hundred years old and has been owned by the same family for seven generations. The former family home with its tower brewery covered in white limewash is now a listed brewer's house with a splendid reception room designed by architect Louis Minard, who was also responsible for the design of the Minard theatre in Ghent. The Bosteels beers: Kwak, Tripel Karmeliet as well as DeuS Brut des Flandres, are difficult to categorise. Kwak is a traditional Belgian top-fermented beer, amber to copper in colour. Tripel Karmeliet is a multi-grain beer inspired by an authentic recipe from 1679 found in the ancient Carmelite monastery in Dendermonde. 'It is not an abbey beer, rather, it is a multi-grain beer containing barley, wheat and oats', Antoine Bosteels explains. The house yeast contributes its special, fruity aroma. Each beer is brewed with a different yeast. 'Beer is very complex', the brewer finds. 'Every single choice you make has consequences. We are making beers with character and try not to emphasise the hop too much. The malt and the yeasts are more important for the taste.' DeuS is the result of a production process that takes several months and is inspired by champagne. The beer is brewed and fermented in Belgium. The DeuS-to-be then travels to France, where it is magically transformed into a sparkling beer using ancient techniques including *remuage* and *dégorgement*. The entire process takes one year. **TIP:** visit Dendermonde, cycle or walk along the dykes of the Scheldt at Vlassenbroek.

Group visits (20 participants and over) available on weekdays by request.

Kerkstraat 92, Buggenhout
+32(0)52/33 23 23 – info@kwak.karmeliet.be
www.bestbelgianspecialbeers.be

CNUDDE

Bizonbier, Cnudde

Brouwerij Cnudde produces limited amounts of Cnudde Oudenaards Bruin and Bizonbier brewed with krieken cherries from the brewer's own orchard. Bizon is a reference to the Ohio bridge across the Scheldt where an American bison stands proudly on each of the bridge heads. The brewery was established in the 1950s and still uses the original equipment. **TIP:** visit Oudenaarde and explore the Flemish Ardennes.

Visits for groups of 15 and over, by arrangement only.

Fabriekstraat 8, Eine (Oudenaarde)
+32(0)55/31 18 34
cnudde.lieven@skynet.be

SINT-NIKLAAS

Things to see and do
- the town hall and the largest market square in the country
- the Cipierage (the old court) and the Oud Parochiehuis (the first town hall)
- the Sint-Nicolaaskerk and its treasures
- the Mercator museum about the history of cartography
- the history of textiles
- the Salon for fine arts
- Walburg Castle
- Moeland Castle and its Egyptian Hall
- the Witte Molen

Tip: explore the Waasland region by bike or on foot or book a balloon flight and discover the city and its surroudings from the air.

Toerisme Sint-Niklaas
Grote Markt 1
+32(0)3/778 30 00
info@sint-niklaas.be
www.sint-niklaas.be

CONTRERAS

Contrapils, Tonneke, Valeir

In the 19th century, a farm, windmill and brewery occupied the highest point in the village of Gavere. The brewery, established in 1818, has been owned by the Contreras family since 1898. Customers used to order a 'tonneke' when beer was still tapped from wooden barrels, hence the name of the house beer. Valeir Extra, a Belgian IPA (India Pale Ale), has an amazing bitterness paired with a zestiness and flowery aromas derived from American hops. A beer that sets itself apart from the rest. **TIP:** walkers can follow the Slag bij Gavereroute or the Aasselkouterroute; by bike, cycle along the Valeirroute or Scheldevalleiroute.

Visit by prior arrangement for groups between 20 and 50 participants.

Molenstraat 110, Gavere
+32(0)9/384 27 06
info@contreras.be
www.contreras.be

DANNY

Kwibus

Danny Hoffelinck launched the Kwibus in a playful reference to little rascals. He started off brewing in his garage but is now running out of space.

Visit by prior arrangement.

Kerkveldstraat 61, Erpe-Mere
+32(0)53/83 58 95
info@brdanny.be
www.brdanny.be

DE RYCK

Arend, Blonde Bladelin, Gouden Arend, Special De Ryck, Steenuilke

In 1886 Gustaaf De Ryck, a tanner, set up his brewery in the heart of Herzele. He had learnt his trade at Zum Goldenen Adler in Bremen, otherwise known as The Golden Eagle. After the First World War the brewery re-opened under a new name: De Ryck. The brewer stuck to brewing top-fermented beers. In 1920 De Ryck introduced an amber beer of the *spéciale belge* type to provide an alternative to pils. For thirty years this was to be the brewery's only beer. A Christmas beer was added in the 1950s, inspired by the British pale ale. This was the predecessor of the Arend Winter. An De Ryck is now brewing artisan beers. Steenuilke ('little owl') was created in support of a bird protection project in the Flemish Ardennes. This beer, enriched with three local herbs, has been incorporated into the standard range. **TIP:** together with the nearby Van den Bossche brewery, De Ryck has set up a two-brewery route called Tussen Pot en Pint (44 or 13 kilometres),.

Visit by prior arrangement for groups of 15-50 participants.

Kerkstraat 24, Herzele
+32(0)53/62 23 02 – info@brouwerijderyck.be
www.brouwerijderyck.be

AALST

Things to see and do
- the belfry, the Schepenhuis (Aldermen's House), the 'gebiedshuisje' (extension to the Town Hall)
- Town Hall and Landhuis
- the Borse van Amsterdam
- Keizersplein square
- 't Gasthuys municipal museum
- the grounds of Terlinden Castle
- the railway station

Tip: take part in the annual Hopdag (Hop Day) on the first Sunday in September, join in the picking at Nedermolenstraat in Meldert and discover the historic importance of hop growing in this region.

Toerisme Aalst
Hopmarkt 51, B-9300 Aalst
+32(0)53/72 38 80
www.aalst.be

DILEWYNS

Vicaris-range

'At the age of 17 I wanted to start brewing but small artisan brewers were a protected species at the time,' Vincent Dilewyns tells us. 'And so I decided to become a dental technician.' In 1998 he started brewing on a small scale. The popularity of his Vicaris Tripel and Generaal was such that he had to enlist the assistance of Lochristi's Proefbrouwerij. Demand kept rising and Vincent decided to start brewing full-time together with his daughters. He is now the owner of a sizeable, well-equipped brewery. Vincent has launched a triple gueuze. 'You can taste and smell the geuze and you also get the mildness of the triple. I am brewing in the traditional way but with modern equipment,' he explains. **TIP:** visit the city of Dendermonde, walk or cycle along the dykes of the Scheldt in Vlassenbroek. Taste the beers in the Sint-Antonius restaurant (www.st-antonius.be) in Grembergen just north of Dendermonde.

Visits on application only, Tuesday to Saturday, for groups of 20-60 participants.

Vlassenhout 5, Dendermonde
+32(0)52/20 18 57 – info@vicaris.be
www.vicaris.be

DONUM IGNIS

Noorderbierke, ZoemZoem, Zuiderbierke

The name of this artisan brewery in the Waasland region literally means 'gift of the fire'. 'Fire' is also a reference to how you can get fired up when drinking. Geert Vertenten teaches maths and chemistry. He has been in the grip of the brewing virus ever since he visited Brasserie d'Achouffe. 'All of my spare time is spent in here', he laughs. The names of two of his beers refer to compass points, a playful reference to the different varieties of malt and hops used for brewing these beers. And ZoemZoem is fragrant with honey. **TIP:** walk or cycle in the green Waasland region.

Phone ahead to arrange your visit.

Leebrugstraat 55, Sinaai-Waas,
+32(0)485/70 76 91
brouwerij@donumignis.be
www.donumignis.be

GLAZEN TOREN (De)

Saison d'Erpe Mere, Ondineke, Jan De Lichte, Cuvée Angélique, Canaster Winterscotch

Jef Van den Steen, a beer author and brewer started up De Glazen Toren brewery in 2004 in partnership with his friends Mark De Neef and Dirk De Pauw. 'It started off as a hobby', Jef Van den Steen tells us. 'Dirk and I were keen home brewers. We decided to work together.' Their Saison d'Erpe-Mere is Aalster's response to the Hainaut *saison*. It was followed by Ondineke, an Aalster triple. Canaster is a brown winter beer. It is named after a former Carmelite monastery and is brewed only once a year on 11 November. Jan De Lichte is a double white beer. And Cuvée Angélique was inspired by the former Cuvée de l'Ermitage from Brasserie de l'Union in Jumet, a *spéciale belge*. De Glazen Toren brews in the traditional way with contemporary equipment. For example, the kettle is heated on a gas burner with one flame only, giving a 'roast' (caramel) taste. Adding boiling water causes the temperature to rise. The brewer prepares a thick mash to intensify the conversion of the malts, leading to drier beers. 'We work with aromatic Hallertau flower hops from Aalst', Jef explains. 'We are refining traditional beers of the people without betraying their character. For example, a *saison* still has to be a good thirstquencher as this is what the beer was intended for.' **TIP:** visit Aalst. Taste the beers in the De Glazen Toren restaurant (www.deglazentoren.be) in Affligem.

Visit by prior arrangement.

> Glazentorenweg 11, Erpe-Mere
> +32(0)53/83 03 80
> info@glazentoren.be
> www.glazentoren.be

DENDERMONDE

Things to see and do
- the Lakenhalle (linen hall) and the belfry
- the beguinage of Sint-Alexius
- the Museum voor Volkskunde (Municipal Folklore Museum)
- Onze-Lieve-Vrouwekerk church
- the Vleeshuismuseum about the history of the city
- Baasrode Maritime Museum
- the Hof Van Peene museum in Baasrode, a former brewery

Tip: walk or cycle along the dykes of the Scheldt in Vlassenbroek.

Toerisme Dendermonde
Stadhuis
Grote Markt, B-9200 Dendermonde
+32(0)52/21 39 56
toerisme@dendermonde.be
www.dendermonde.be

GRAAL (De)

De Graal

Brouwerij De Graal is a recently established, artisan brewery in the heart of the Flemish Ardennes. Much of the brewing done by Wim Saeyens is commissioned by other brewers. Whenever he is working with herbs and spices, he aims for the perfect dosage. The beer has to be balanced after all. Wim: 'I am a chemist and so I am used to using precise measurements. As a brewer, you also need this precision.' **TIP:** take a hike or a bike ride in the Flemish Ardennes (www.toerismevlaamseardennen.be).

Visit by prior arrangement for groups of between 10 and 30 participants. The doors are open to smaller groups and individual visitors every Saturday between 0900 and 1600.

Industrielaan 42A, Brakel
+32(0)494/71 87 29
www.degraal.be

GRUUT (Stadsbrouwerij)

Ghentse Gruutbieren

The Gruut city brewery lies right in the heart of Ghent. Annick De Splenter, the brewer, uses a herbal mixture called 'gruit' instead of hops. In the Middle Ages the River Leie divided the city of Ghent into two administrative parts. The right bank was subject to German rule and the brewers here used German hop varieties from the 13th century onwards. The French were in charge on the left bank where the brewers used gruit. Landowners imposed beer taxes which depended on the quantity of herbs used. Every region had its own blend of herbs. The landowner was aware of the mixture used and levied his taxes accordingly. 'Gruut' is also what the locals called the 'groot', the currency in use during the reign of Emperor Charles V, which came in single and double coins. After gruit was replaced by hops the coins remained in circulation. The gruut coin now forms part of the logo of this city brewery. For her beers, Annick De Splenter pairs modern brewing technology with ancient tradition. **TIP:** visit Ghent's historic city centre.

Day visit free of charge every day until 1800 hours. Groups comprising 8-100 participants need to book ahead.

Rembert Dodoensdreef, Ghent
+32(0)9/269 02 69
info@gruut.be
www.gruut.be

GERAARDSBERGEN

Things to see and do
- the iconic Muur van Geraardsbergen and its cobblestones that form an indelible part of the Tour of Flanders cycle race
- Oudenberg chapel
- the Town Hall and the oldest Manneken Pis in the country
- the Church of St. Bartholomew
- the Marbol fountain

Tip: sample a slice of 'mattentaart', a Geraardsbergen specialty, and take part in the annual Krakelingenworp and Tonnekensbrand parade at the end of February.

Toerisme Geraardsbergen
Markt
B-9500 Geraardsbergen
+32(0)54/43 72 89
toerisme@Geraardsbergen.be
www.Geraardsbergen.be

↓ Ghent, Graslei

HUYGHE

Artevelde, Averbode, Blanche des Neiges, Campus, Delirium, Floris, La Guillotine, Mongozo, St. Idesbald, Villers

In 1902 Léon Huyghe started a brewery and named it after himself. Huyghe, known for its Delirium Tremens – the pink elephant beer – also brews abbey beers, pils beers, classic top-fermented beers, beers with exotic tastes, regional specialties and organic, fair trade and gluten free beers. 'We don't like to pigeonhole ourselves', admits Alain De Laet, Managing Director. 'We established our reputation with the slogan "You ask, we brew". Our engineers have mastered the art of brewing and are capable of using almost any ingredient. They can produce fair trade beers (Mongozo Quinua, Banana, Mango, Coconut and so on) as well as chocolate beer, orange-coloured pils or heavier beers that re-ferment in the bottle.' The characteristic taste of Delirium comes from three different varieties of yeast. The quirky packaging in bottles painted in white with colourful labels, is another factor in Delirium's success. The label depicts the various stages of intoxication. The pink elephant has now embarked on a life of its own. Huyghe is a top exporter. Its beers are sold to 93 countries around the world. **TIP:** visit Ghent's historic city centre or take a bike ride on the dykes of the River Scheldt between Melle and Ghent.

Brewery tours are available by prior arrangement for groups of at least 15 participants. There is a brewery museum that displays items from the archives and an extensive collection of vintage beer advertising and brewing equipment right down to a café from the 1930s complete with fixtures and fittings. Brouwerij Huyghe opened a range of themed Delirium cafés in Getrouwheidsgang just off Korte Beenhouwersstraat in Brussels as well as far beyond Belgium's borders.

Brusselsesteenweg 282, Melle
+32(0)9/252 15 01 – jose.debock@telenet.be
www.delirium.be
Delirium Café, Getrouwheidsgang 4, Brussels
+32(0)2/514 44 34 – www.deliriumcafe.be

GHENT

Things to see and do
- St. Bavo Cathedral and the triptych The Adoration of the Lamb of God, painted by the Van Eyck brothers
- the City Hall and the Belfry
- Graslei and Korenlei
- the market squares
- St. Michael's bridge for its views of this medieval city
- Gravensteen (the Castle of the Counts) and the medieval Patershol quarter
- SMAK, the Museum of Contemporary Arts
- the Museum of Fine Arts
- the STAM Museum about the City of Ghent
- the Alijnhuis, a museum displaying popular art
- the Vooruit Arts Centre
- the beguinages
- the beautifully lit historic city centre
- the Oude Dokken (Old Docks) at Dampoort, a creative hotspot

Tip: visit Ghent at the time of the annual Ghentse Feesten, the largest city festival in Europe, in the third week of July.

Visit Gent
Oude Vismijn
Sint-Veerleplein 5
B-9000 Ghent
+32(0)9/266 56 60
visit@ghent.be
www.visitgent.be

Ghent, Graslei

OUDENAARDE

Things to see and do
- the Town Hall with its belfry and Grote Markt
- Sint-Walburgakerk
- the Carillon with its regular concerts
- the Boudewijntoren and Huis Margaretha van Parma
- the Centrum Ronde van Vlaanderen about the Tour of Flanders
- the beguinage
- the Pamele quarter
- the archaeological site of the abbey of Ename, known for its abbey beer

Tip: the Flemish Ardennes are made for a hike or a bike ride

Toerisme Oudenaarde
Town Hall
+32(0)55/31 72 51
www.oudenaarde.be
www.toerismevlaamseardennen.be

KROONTJE ('t)

Rebelle beers

In 2000 Marc Verberckmoes, the son of a well-known beer merchant from Elversele, and Dimitri Verbraekel, an avid label collector and colleague, opened a microbrewery. Before long they had brewed a brown beer, then a little blonde... Where does the name come from? Denderbelle, where the brewery is located, is popularly known as 'Belle'.

Microbrewery. Contact the brewery prior to your visit.

Hogebrug 62, Denderbelle
+32(0)495/43 33 25
contact@tkroontje.be
www.tkroontje.be

LIEFMANS

Liefmans Fruitesse, Goudenband, Kriek Brut & Oud Bruin

The Liefmans brewery on the banks of the Scheldt is a living museum. The original brewing equipment is well preserved. A visit shows you the amount of manual work required by traditional brewing techniques. The unique taste of Liefmans beers comes from the mixed fermentation in open fermentation basins, the extra-long cold storage (for up to three years in chilled barrels), the use of real krieken cherries and the blending of young and old beer. Why did people start blending beers? Beer that had been brewed in the winter had to keep until the summer. Older beers are 'cut' with younger, fresher and sweeter beer to renew their taste. The beer re-ferments after mixing and acquires a more balanced and consistent taste. Liefmans beer is brewed with light, dark and roast malts. It ferments for a week before spending four to eight months in the warm chambers. Kriekbier is made on the basis of the brown beer type. The krieken cherries are steeped in young beer for up to half a year and the 'kriekbier' produced is once again cut with older beer. This brewery has always made an effort to use Belgian ingredients wherever possible. The krieken provide a great example: all of the cherries used in the Kriek Brut are sourced from the Haspengouw region. A deliberate choice. The sour cherries are mixed with blond beer straight after harvesting and this mixture will remain untouched for at least a year and a half. It is left up to the 'krieken' (sour cherries) to release their juices. The yeasts and bacteria nestling in the pores of the copper equipment provide the characteristic lactic acid taste of brown beer from Oudenaarde. **TIP:** Oudenaarde is well worth a visit.

Guided visits for 15 to 35 people. Reservations are necessary.

Aalststraat 200, Oudenaarde
+32(0)3/860 94 00 – info@liefmans.be
www.liefmans.be

MALHEUR (De Landtsheer)

Malheur-range, Novice-range

Malheur is brewed at De Landtsheer in Buggenhout. The brewery in its current form saw the light in 1997. 'We started off with a clean slate', Manu De Landtsheer tells us. 'That's when we launched the Malheur name. This brewery used to produce sour beers. In my grandfather's days there was no formal brewing education and no regular source of yeast.' Herbs and spices are not used for the blond beers but they are ingredients for the brown beers. All of our beers are living, unpasteurised beers that re-ferment in the bottle and the barrel. The taste evolves throughout the years and as a consequence, beers with a different age will vary. Brouwerij Malheur established its reputation with its Brut beers. The brewer's intention is to elevate beer to a gastronomic level. Malheur Bière Brut, an exclusive and rich beer, re-ferments in the bottle for a third time. The brewer has developed a procedure whereby the yeast is collected in the neck of the bottle. This yeast is subsequently frozen and, as part of a process called disgorging or *dégorgement*, the frozen yeast plug is removed; a process also used for champagne. The result is a refined and sparkling beer with a robust head and an elegant finish, suitable both as an aperitif and a thirstquencher. The Brut beers take a very long time to produce. 'We are now experimenting with a new beer style using dry hopping to enhance the aroma (citrus, grapefruit, wine...).'

Book ahead for a tour, weekdays only.

Mandekensstraat 179, Buggenhout
+32(0)52/33 39 11
info@malheur.be
www.malheur.be

PAENHUYS ('t)

Kloefkapper, Puitenkop, Schapenkop, Zwarte Zjef

'"'t Paenhuys", refers to a place full of pans and kettles used for brewing beer', Paul Van Nieulande, the brewer, explains. 'Every village used to have its own "paenhuys". At Bokrijk Open Air Museum you can see an authentic pan house from Diepenbeek (see: Genk region for Things to see and do). My dream is that one day, every single village will have its own 'pan house'. Paul's first two beers go under the names of Zwarte Zjef en 't Paenhuys Tripel. Zwarte Zjef pays homage to a legendary liquorice seller in Beveren who came to Belgium from Africa. **TIP:** take a stroll around Sint-Niklaas or take a hike or a bike ride to explore the green Waasland region (www.toerismewaasland.be).
Phone or email ahead to arrange your visit.

Nieuwkerkenstraat 202b, Nieuwkerke-Waas
+32(0)475/70 10 01 – paul.vn@telenet.be
www.tpaenhuys.be

ROMAN

Adriaen Brouwer, Ename-bieren, Ghentse Strop, Mater, Rebelse Strop, Romy Pils, Sloeber

The oldest family brewery in the country is located in the heart of the Flemish Ardennes. 'We have been brewing here ever since 1545', Carlo Roman, General Manager, tells us. Carlo represents the fifteenth generation of this brewing dynasty. The origins of the Roman brewery go back as far as the De Clocke inn, located on a main road between Germany and France. Until 1604 Joos Roman was the bailiff of the Schorisse region as well as boss at the inn. Joos was a contemporary of Adriaen Brouwer, a painter and artist from Oudenaarde, best known for his depictions of tavern life. Roman named his beer after this illustrious hedonist. 'Bruin, dobbel bruin, tafelbier en export' ('Brown, double brown, table beer and export') were noted in the brewbook just after the Second World War. The export beer turned out to be the predecessor of Romy Pils, in high demand in all of the cafés in Oudenaarde and far beyond. 'Pils was a new departure for us; beforehand, we had a long tradition of brown beer'. The 1980s saw the advent of specialty beers. Sloeber was Roman's first strong blond beer. 'For us, it was an initation into stronger beers that re-ferment in the bottle', the brewer explains. In 1989 Sloeber was followed by Ename abbey beer. 'We found our inspiration for an abbey beer when we attended an open air performance at the Ename abbey ruins'. Ename has now been incorporated into the municipality of Oudenaarde. In 1064 the Benedictines established themselves in this village in a former fortified castle (973). The oldest traces of brewing activity on the site go all the way back to the 11th century. However, Ename shares its fate with that of most of the abbeys in our country: it was razed to the ground during the French Revolution. All that remains is the beer. Gentse Strop (2011) is a reminder of this historic tie between the cities of Oudenaarde and Ghent. The main part is played by Emperor Charles V who was born in Ghent. His daughter, Margaret of Parma, was born (out of wedlock) in Oudenaarde. And this is where beer enters the story. Legend has it that, when Hanske De Krijger ('Hanske the Warrior') was keeping watch, he fell asleep as he had overindulged in the local beer. He failed to notice the Emperor and his troops invading Oudenaarde. Hanske is now the emblem of the city. And the 'strop', or noose? This was used to punish the rebellious Ghent citizens. The Emperor forced the dignitaries of the city to wear a noose around their necks as they had been opposing his reign. The inhabitants of Ghent have been known as 'stroppendragers', or 'noose bearers' ever since. **TIP:** visit Oudenaarde, cycle or walk in the Flemish Ardennes (www.toerismevlaamseardennen.be). Arrange your visit in advance if your group comprises 15 and over. A guaranteed tour is held every Saturday from early March to end October. **TIP:** in July, concerts are staged on Wednesday evenings.

Hauwaert 105, Mater (Oudenaarde)
+32(0)55/45 54 01 – visit@roman.be
www.roman.be

↑ Oudenaarde, beguinage

↓ Oudenaarde, town hall

SINT CANARUS

De Maeght van Gottem, Potteloereke, Sint Canarus Tripel

One of the smallest breweries around was born in 1988. It was set up with an old laundry tub. In 1999 Sint Canarus moved into a cottage in Gottem. Sign up to a beer seminar and Doctor Canarus will tell you all you need to know about beer and brewing in general. On the menu: the history of Sint Canarus, the theory and practice of beer tasting, answers to often-asked questions such as how beer is made, who drinks beer and how much do they drink, the history of beer and the relationship between beer and health.

The brewery welcomes visitors every Sunday between 1100 and 2100. Phone ahead for a group visit.

Polderweg 2, Gottem (Deinze)
+32(0)51/63 69 31 info@sintcanarus.be
www.sintcanarus.be

NINOVE

Things to see and do
- the Onze-Lieve-Vrouw Hemelvaartabdijkerk
- the archeological abbey site
- the old town hall
- the Koepoort (Cowgate)
- the valley of the river Dender
- Neigembos nature reserve

Toerisme Ninove
Centrumlaan 100
B-9400 Ninove
+32(0)54/31 32 85
www.ninove.be

SLAGHMUYLDER

Ambiorix, Kerstbier, Paasbier, Slag-pils, Witkap-range, Wortelbier

Emmanuel Slaghmuylder was a grain trader who established this brewery in 1860. The latter part of his surname, 'muylder', translates as 'miller' and points to his original trade. The fifth generation is now at the helm of this brewery. They inherited the Witkap beers from the now defunct De Drie Linden brewery from Brasschaat. The Witkap name refers to the white hoods worn by Cistercian monks but, surprisingly, is not related to a local abbey. 'Some time ago we acquired an existing but ailing brand and we hit the jackpot,' Luc Verhaegen, the owner, explains. Witkap Stimulo has turned into a reference amongst blonde beers. Quite a light beer, subtly bitter, with a freshly sour and flowery taste.' Slaghmuylder also produces Slag pils, only distributed in Ninove. **TIP:** Ninove is worth a visit.

Visit by prior arrangement for groups of 20 and over.

Denderhoutembaan 2, Ninove – +32(0)54/33 18 31
info@witkap.be – www.witkap.be

SMISJE

Big Bayou, Smiske

Johan Brandt, a printer, has been running his brewery in Mater near Oudenaarde since 2008. 'This is the former site of the Amelberga lemonade factory, which was named after one of the 25 recognised springs in Flanders,' Johan tells us. We use the water from this spring plus water drawn from a well. Beers like Guido, Wostijntje (made with mustard seed also used by the well-known Wostyn mustard factory in Torhout), Imperial Stout Catherine, Smisje Speciaal with pumpkin seed, Smisje Plus dubbel IPA and Kuvée Elektrik all linger in the taste memory. But the brewer has pared down the assortment quite drastically. The range now comprises only a handful of beers including Smiske. Johan has made a promise to take one of his beers back into production each year if he receives sufficient moral support on Facebook. He is keen on innovation. For example, at the 2011 Zythos Bierfestival in Sint-Niklaas Johan launched the Hop Randall. This is produced using a water filter filled with hop flowers. Johan: 'We install it between the barrel and the tap so the beer, when it is poured, undergoes an *instant dry hopping*.' **TIP**: visit Oudenaarde, take a hike or a bike ride in the Flemish Ardennes.

Visits need to be arranged in advance for groups of between 20 and a maximum of 49, Monday – Friday. The brewery café is open every Sunday, May to October from 1500 to 1900 hours, with a guided tour at 1400.

Driesleutelstraat 1, Mater (Oudenaarde)
+32(0)475/36 44 89 – visitsmisje@hotmail.com
www.smisje.be

TSEUT (Den)

Belle Cies, Bras, Den Bi3r, Den Drupneuze, Den Mulder, Den Krulsteirt, Den Tseut, Hoppesnoet, 't Wijveke, 't Zeemken

The small craft home brewery of Den Tseut lies at the centre of the village. 'Tseut' means 'pig' in local dialect. Oosteeklo is known for its pig farming. Den Tseut started brewing in 2008. **TIP:** take a ride along one of the three local bike routes: Den Tseut, Den Mulder or Den Bi3r.

Phone or email ahead to arrange a group visit (maximum 25 participants). The small brewery café is open Saturdays (1400 to 2130 hours) and Sundays (1600 to 2130 hours).

Oosteeklo-Dorp 40, Assenede
+32(0)485/37 20 11
huisbrouwerij.den.tseut@telenet.be
www.huisbrouwerijdentseut.be

VAN DEN BOSSCHE

Buffalo, Pater Lieven, Livinus & Lamoral Degmont

Did you know that, in 1907, Buffalo Bill's circus once put up its tent in Ghent at the site of the KAA Gent football stadium? This is why its supporters are nicknamed the Buffalos. At the time, the brewing staff took a trip to the circus whilst the wort was boiling. They paid a boy to keep an eye on the fire underneath the brewing kettle during the performance. The boy did a good job firing the kettle but had not stirred the wort enough. The wort got slightly burnt in the process but was still used for fermentation. This little accident resulted in a heavier beer with touches of caramel. Buffalo is now brewed with roast malts and caramel malts. Buffalo is a dark, top-fermented beer that lies halfway between a sweet scotch and a bitter stout. Buffalo Belgian Stout is a version that has matured on Bordeaux barrels, a vinous beer that re-ferments in the bottle. Bruno Van den Bossche puts it this way: 'You smell a red wine and you taste oak.' In 1897 Arthur Van den Bossche started up his brewery at the village square of Sint-Lievens-Esse. The fourth generation of brewers is now at the helm. Bruno is in charge of sales and his brother Emmanuel does the brewing. 'Our Pater Lieven is a playful reference to an Irish monk', Bruno tells us about this other flagship beer in the Van den Bossche range. 'This monk crossed the sea to convert the locals to the Christian faith and paid for it with his life. However, this man of God was not discouraged. With his head under his arm he made his way to Sint-Lievens-Houtem. Wherever he put down his stick, springs would well up. Wouldn't every brewer like to do this? ' The Buffalo Belgian Stout pairs subtle touches of roast coffee with a slightly sweet taste. Right on target. **TIP:** the 'two brewery' cycle route named 'Tussen Pot en Pint', initiated by the De Ryck and Van den Bossche breweries. Another option for cyclists is the Livinusroute. Visit by prior arrangement only for groups of 20 and over.

Sint-Lievensplein 16, Sint-Lievens-Esse (Herzele)
+32(0)54/50 04 11 – info@paterlieven.be
www.paterlieven.be

VAN STEENBERGE

Augustijn, Bornem, Celis White, Gulden Draak, Leute Bokbier, Piraat, St. Stefanus

This is the only large brewery in the historical Meetjesland region. In 1978 the Augustine monks from Ghent knocked on the brewer's door and Augustijn beer has been produced in Evergem ever since. In the Middle Ages, the monks themselves brewed and sold the beer, in times when beer was an alternative for water. De Gulden Draak pays homage to the gilded statue at the top of the Belfry of the City of Ghent. Gulden Draak beer is different from Van Steenberge's usual range as it re-ferments with a wine yeast, turning it into a barley wine. It used to be an occasional, celebratory beer commissioned by the mayor of a nearby village. His Italian guests tasted it, liked it and urged the brewer to continue brewing it. The striking white bottle was hand-painted at first but is now covered with a sleeve. The Gulden Draak Quadrupel 9000 is another beer that arose from coincidence, when the brewer forgot to add caramel malt. Van Steenberge was one of the first brewers to experiment with in-bottle re-fermentation in the 1960s. They are now using nine different yeast cultures. **TIP:** combine your visit with a trip to the Augustine Monastery in Ghent from which the Augustijn abbey beers derive their name. Also explore the picturesque Meetjesland region and the Krekenroute bike trail. Stop off for a specialty beer at Huyze Vacas in the town of Waterland-Oudeman.

Brewery tours on Monday, Tuesday and Wednesday. By pre-arrangement only, for groups between 8 and 30.

Lindenlaan 25, Ertvelde (Evergem)
+32(0)9/344 50 71
info@vansteenberge.com
www.vansteenberge.com

TOERISME OOST-VLAANDEREN
Sint-Niklaasstraat 2
B-9000 Ghent
+32(0)9/269 26 00
toerisme@oost-vlaanderen.be
www.tov.be

GENK
HASSELT
MAASEIK
SINT-TRUIDEN
TONGEREN

ACHELSE KLUIS
(De) (Benedictine abbey)

Achel

I meet with Brother Charles. He is not really qualified to comment on the Trappist beer as he does not touch alcohol, but puts a call out for the brewmaster. The eyes of Brother Charles light up with fun. 'A lot of devotion and a lot of pleasure', he grins whilst showing me the Laurel and Hardy DVDs someone has just sent him. 'But I'm not one for modern film or television', he modestly admits. In his company, any trace of stress just melts away. Brother Charles, on the phone: 'Business is a big word to use, we are an abbey here!' I learn that these brothers were brewing beer even before the First World War. However, the Germans chased them away and requisitioned the copper equipment. Achel co-operates closely with the Westmalle abbey brewery. 'We are improving all the time', the brewer explains. 'We carve out our own paths but have regular discussions with our fellow monks. All of us Trappists produce our own beers. Why should we ape each other?' I enjoy a drink here with a sound conscience as a proportion of every Trappist sold goes to charity. So, who signed his name to the Achel recipe? At first there was Brother Thomas from Westmalle, followed by Brother Antoine from Rochefort... Let's go back in time for just a minute. In the year 1846, 27 Trappist monks from Westmalle established themselves in Achel. They built workhouses, a gatehouse and a guest wing and converted the prayer chapel of the former hermits into a church. For over a hundred years, the monks were at the forefront of sustainable agriculture, cattle farming and trades (bakery, carpentry, printing, copper beating, cart making and forging iron). In 1989 they sold the majority of their agricultural lands. Achel is now a green oasis emanating peace and quiet. **TIP 1:** the abbey of De Achelse Kluis lies in a green belt but is close to the cycling route network, the moors of the Leenderhei, the forests of Hamont-Achel and a tourist driving route close to the Dutch border. Hikes in the Achel area can be found on www.wandelroutes.org.

TIP 2: explore the Trappistenwandelroutes (4.2–12.8 km).

This Trappist abbey and its brewery are not open to visitors. The abbey tavern and its interior court do afford a view of the brewing kettles, allowing you to follow the brewing process through a glass wall. Tip: taste the Grevenbroecker blue-veined cheese, produced by Catharinadal, and visit the dairy where it is made (www.catharinadal.be).

Kluis 1, Hamont-Achel
+32(0)11/80 07 60
www.achelsekluis.org

ALKEN-MAES

Brugs Witbier, Ciney, Cristal, Maes Pils, GrimMons, Hapkin, Judas, Op-Ale, Postel

Cristal is the most popular pils in Limburg province. Every second Limburg café has Cristal on tap. The original recipe, devised in 1928, still lies at the basis of the quality and taste of this pils. Cristal is one of the bitterest pils beers in Belgium. The Alken brewery set out to quench the thirst of Belgian miners in the 1920s and 1930s. The month of May in the year 1928 has made an indelible mark on Belgian beer history: this Limburg brewery introduced its Cristal pils. At the time, this beer was nothing short of revolutionary, as not many Belgian breweries were able to brew bottom-fermented beers. Cristal Alken makes the most of the Limburg feeling. In the Province of Limburg, you'd order a 'Cristalleke' rather than a pint. The current brewery, established in 1924, was the first in Limburg to produce bottom-fermented beers. Cristal is brewed with soft water that is calcium and mineral free. It is delicately hopped (Czech - Saaz) and easy to digest. This pils owes its delicate flavour and clear colour to its pairing of malt and maize. **TIP:** explore this green Limburg region on foot or by bike and make time to enjoy a 'Cristalleke'. We recommend Café Sportwereld in the heart of Alken.

Book your tour of the Alken-Maes brewery in advance. After the tour, pop into Het Moment, the village café right next to the brewery.

Stationsstraat 2, Alken
+32(0)11/59 03 06 – info@alken-maes.com
www.alken-maes.be
www.hetmomentalken.be

AMAI

Loemelaer beers

Henk Fijneman, a fireman, brews the Loemelaer fully malted beers in his spare time. His microbrewery lays claim to the title of the 'smallest brewery in Belgium'. Seeing and tasting is believing, You can choose between a blonde, a brown beer, a tripel and a Russian Imperial Stout. Henk likes to experiment with various hops, use techniques like *dry hopping* and is brave enough to use wild yeasts. There is plenty of opportunity for walking in the Lommelse Sahara or Bosland nature reserves. Lommel offers a great range of holiday parks. **TIP:** taste the beers at Cuchara, a gastronomic restaurant (www.cuchara.be).

Visit by prior arrangement. And pop into De Kroon (1902), a café typical of the Kempen region, in Lommel.

Konijnenpijp 11, Lommel
+32(0)472/17 02 20 – www.brouwerij-amai.be

AMBURON BELGIAN CRAFTBREWERY

Tungri beers

This brewery, on the edge of the city of Tongeren, is passionate about the history of its home city. 'Amburon' refers to Ambiorix, the chief of the local Eburones tribe, who staged a successful fight against the Roman occupiers. The Tungri are the original inhabitants of Tongeren, Belgium's most ancient city. Amburon's mission is to produce beers that pay homage to tradition, not extreme but nevertheless with a pure taste, balanced and accessible. Examples include the refreshing and fruity Tungri Bitter and the very quaffable, mild Tungri Blond triple. **TIP:** sightseeing in Tongeren, the oldest city in the country.

Tours have to be arranged in advance. Take in the sights of the city before or after your visit.

Hasseltsesteenweg 617, Tongeren
+32(0)496/02 24 58
davy@amburonbelgiancraftbrewery.be
www.tungri.eu

CORNELISSEN (Dorpsbrouwerij)

Bokkereyer, Bosbier, Herkenrode, Kriekenbier, Limburgse Witte, Ops-Ale, Pax, Sint-Gummarus

'My grandfather established the first real brewhall with its own fermentation chambers here in the 1930s. They are in use up to this day', brewer Jef Cornelissen tells us. The Sint-Jozef brewery, now re-named Cornelissen, traces its 1804 origins back to a farm, just like many other breweries. The recipe for Ops-Ale has remained virtually unchanged throughout the years. The water is drawn from a well 180 metres deep. They are still using the same hop variety. The only difference is that maize starch has been replaced with wheat starch. The yeast strain is the same as ever. After fermentation the beer goes into cold storage for four to

TONGEREN

Things to see and do
- the Markt and the City Hall
- the Basilica, the cloisters and the Teseum with its church treasures
- the Moerenpoort, a medieval city gate, and
- the medieval city walls
- the beguinage and its museum
- the Gallo-Roman museum and the Roman city fortifications
- the antiques market on Sunday morning
- the castle domain of the Grand Commandery of Alden Biesen

Tip: follow the Mijlpaalroutes (milestone trails) signposted in red, blue or green and the coloured letter M and visit the annual Ambierorix Bierfestival held in the first weekend of August (see: beer festivals).

Toerisme Tongeren
Via Julianus, Julianus Shopping
B-3700 Tongeren
+32(0)12/80 00 70
www.tongeren.be

five weeks and is then filtered. Ops-Ale is a local product that is tapped and poured in cafés in the area. This quality pils owes much to German brewing tradition. Bokkereyer takes us back to the 18th century when this region was plagued by bandits. These 'bokkenrijders' (*buck riders*) flew through the air, riding the back of a goat, or buck, to escape the long arm of the law. This legend lives on in a mild, full-mouthed amber beer. **TIP:** take the bike or go on a hike in the province of Noord-Limburg and explore the Kempen-Broek nature reserve.

Visit by prior arrangement for groups of 10 and over. Have a drink and a bite to eat at the village square.

> Itterplein 19, Opitter (Bree)
> +32(0)89/86 47 11
> info@brouwerijcornelissen.be
> www.brouwerijcornelissen.be

ENGILSEN

Dief! Copper, Dief! Gold, Dief! Silver

Frederik Gils, a biological engineer, is busy brewing his Dief!. His love of LaChouffe provided the necessary inspiration. Dief...? The name of this beer translates as 'thief' and this brewery's zesty blonde, tripel and quadrupel are guaranteed to steal your heart. Taste them in a range of local cafés. **TIP:** visit the Beringen mine museum, the Gerhagen nature reserve, the estates of Merode and the small city of Diest and its beguinage.

Open every Thursday night between 1900 and 2100 or by prior arrangement.

> Lindenstraat 36, Tessenderlo
> +32(0)13/29 58 21
> info@brouwerijengilsen.be
> www.brouwerijengilsen.be

MAASEIK

Things to see and do
- the Market Square
- the Kruisherenkerk (Crusaders' Church)
- Sint-Catharinakerk and its treasures
- the apothecary museum herb garden
- the Regionaal Archeologisch Museum Regional Archaeological Museum
- the water mills along the Bosbeek and Oeterbeek streams

Tip: cycle along the Meuse and admire its little villages or else, take a boat trip to the small town of Thorn, just across the border with the Netherlands, famous for its white houses.

Toerisme Maaseik
Markt 1, B-3680 Maaseik
+32(0)89/81 92 90
www.toerisme.maaseik.be

↓ Herkenrode

JESSENHOFKE

Arvum, Brown, Maya, Pimpernel, Regular, Reserva, Tripel

IT worker Gert Jordens started off as a hobby brewer in 2000 when he developed his first organic beer, the Jessenhofke Tripel. A Hasselt-based producer of seitan (wheat gluten) provides a protein-rich substitute for Italian wheat. Gert Jordens: 'The water they use for rinsing the seitan serves as the brewing water for our blond Maya beer. We use the bran in our bread. My malt comes from Mamberg in Germany, the hops come from Poperinge and the water is sourced from a spring in France. We collect rain water to cool down our brewing kettles.' Arvum is a beer with a minimum impact on the environment, brewed with barley cultivated in the grounds of the former abbey of Herkenrode. Another Arvum beer is based on malt smoked on chips made from cuttings of apple trees. The raw barley provides the sour touch. Jessenhofke procures its honey from the city beekeeper of Hasselt.
TIP: a great destination for cyclists, not far from either Hasselt or Herkenrode.

Contact the brewery to arrange your visit. Brewing workshops are held regularly.

> Simpernelstraat 17, Hasselt
> +32(0)11/25 56 99 – info@jessenhofke.be
> www.jessenhofke.be

KERKOM

Adelardus, Bink, Bloesem Kriek, Hop Verdomme IPA, Kerckomse Triple, Winterkoninkske

A farm established in 1878 in an idyllic location nestled within the cherry orchards of Sint-Truiden. Marc Limet goes for beers with plenty of character such as the Bink Blond, a traditional Belgian bitter. Also sample the Bink cheese, made with the same beer. 'We make honest products with a pure taste', Marc assures us. We agree with him wholeheartedly. **TIP:** at Sint-Truiden, visit the abbey grounds and the beguinage, take a bike ride or a walk around the fruit region of Haspengouw, especially when the trees are in blossom.

Individual visits every Saturday afternoon at 1500 from March to October. Groups of 10 and over are welcome by prior arrangement.

> Naamsesteenweg 469, Kerkom (Sint-Truiden)
> +32(0)11/68 20 87 of +32(0)495/38 12 14,
> info@brouwerijkerkom
> www.brouwerijkerkom.be

HASSELT

Things to see and do
- Grote Markt
- the beguinage
- Sint-Quintinuskathedraal and its clock tower
- the National Jenever Museum
- the Modemuseum (Fashion Museum)
- the Japanse Tuin (Japanese Garden)
- Kiewit nature reserve
- the grounds of the former abbey of Herkenrode (see: Things to see and do)

Tip: follow the 'Smaakroute', or Taste Trail.

Visit Hasselt
Maastrichterstraat 59
3500 Hasselt
+32(0)11/23 95 40
www.visithasselt.be

MARTENS

Martens Pils, Sezoens, Kristoffel Witbier

Brouwerij Martens, founded in 1758, is primarily known for its Sezoens, a golden-coloured beer with a remarkably hoppy character. Martens produces pils on a large scale. In 2007 a second pils brewery became operational in Kaulille.

The brewery is not open to visitors, However, straight across from the brewery you will find the Bocholter Brouwerijmuseum (see: Things to see and do). Brouwerij Martens provided the impetus for this museum.

Reppelerweg 1, Bocholt
+32(0)89/47 29 80 – www.martens.be

PERRON BIEREN

Boegetbier, Perron Blond Sorachi Ace, Saison Mandarina Bavaria

Light beers with plenty of taste thanks to the use of aromatic hops grown by the brewer himself. That is the trademark of this young microbrewery owned by Jasper Dijkers. The name 'perron' was chosen in homage to the symbol of the liberty of the city that can be found in Liège, Maaseik, Tongeren and Bilzen. 'Backyard hops', stated on the label of several Perron beers, refers to the brewery's own hop field in the garden. *Saison* and the winter beer always form part of the menu which also includes beers intended for a particular season. **TIP:** in the vicinity you can explore the Hoge Kempen nature reserve and the picturesque village of Oud-Rekem on the banks of the River Meuse, where you can taste the beers in café De Sjilder (www.desjilder-oudrekem.be).

Visit by prior arrangement for groups of 8 and over.

Houterstraat 72, Gellik (Lanaken)
+32(0)468/20 82 86 – info@perronbieren.be
www.perronbieren.be

TER DOLEN (Kasteelbrouwerij)

Ter Dolen Armand, Blond, Donker, Kriek, Tripel & Winter

Mieke Desplenter, who owns Ter Dolen, tells her story sitting by the open fire in the brewery café. 'At the end of 1993 I purchased this dilapidated castle and its farmhouse from former Prime Minister Duvieusart', Mieke reveals. 'The renovations took nine months before we could move in.' The brewery is housed in one of the handsome gatehouses that surround the interior court. Until the French Revolution, Ter Dolen served as a refuge for the abbots of Sint-Truiden. The coat of arms above one of the doors in the brewery is reminiscent of those times. The castle-farm cum brewery are now a magnet for tourists. 'At Ter Dolen we only brew recognised abbey beers and, what's more, in buildings that once formed part of an abbey – and that is quite unusual in our country', Mieke assures us. Regional beers from Limburg province, that is the trademark. **TIP:** visit the mining site of Houthalen-Helchteren, Domein Kelchterhoef, Molenheide or the open air museum at Bokrijk.

Guided tours are held at 1500 on Saturday and Sunday. Groups of 15 and over are asked to arrange their visit in advance. Tip: stay overnight in the idyllic Paenhoeve (www.depaenhoeve.be) in Eksel, a B&B run by Mieke's sister Inge, and book a 'brouwersarrangement' (brewer's package).

Eikendreef 21, Helchteren-Houthalen
+32(0)11/60 69 99
info@terdolen.be
www.terdolen.be

GENK

Things to see and do
- KRC Genk football stadium and the Goalmine experience centre
- Bokrijk open air museum (see: Worth a detour?)
- C-Mine, a former mining site, now a design Mecca
- The tunnels of Winterslag mine at in C-Mine
- the studio of ceramic artist Pieter Stockmans
- Thor park in Waterschei, with a focus on technology
- the garden neighbourhoods of Waterschei,
- Winterslag and Zwartberg
- the former mining sites and cités
- De Hoge Kempen nature reserve
- the fresh produce market at Vennestraat in
- Winterslag close to C-Mine
- the Mijnmuseum at Beringen and the unique industrial heritage site

Tip: download the Mijnverhaal (Mi(ne) Story) app (free via Play Store or the App Store).

Visit Genk
C-mine 10 bus 2
3600 Genk
+32(0)89/65 44 90
www.visitgenk.be

TOETËLÈR (Den)

Toetëlèr Amber Tripel, Echte Kriek, Speculaas, Special & Witbier

'We were able to brew in het Paenhuys at Bokrijk open air museum (see Things to See and Do); an unforgettable experience. This is where we learnt the ancient brewing techniques which lie at the heart of the way we brew today,' Luc Festjens explains. He is often joined by two friends to brew in a former car garage. The flagship beer, called Toetëlèr, is a white beer with elderflower. 'Toetëlèr' is Hoeselt dialect for the elder tree. The old wood is hollow and was commonly used to make whistles and tooting horns. You will also taste an amber triple and a kriek based on white beer. **TIP:** explore the nature around Hoeselt, visit the Gallo-Roman museum at Tongeren or the castle of Alden Biesen.

Visit on request for groups between 6 and 25 participants.

Kleistraat 54, Hoeselt
+32(0)89/41 70 85 of +32(0)472/80 24 14
info@toeteler.be
www.toeteler.be

WILDEREN

Cuvée Clarisse, Wilderen Goud, Wilderen Kriek, Tripel Kanunnik

'Let's make clear first of all that we are not a museum. What you can do at our new site is go for a walk through time. We accompany the visitor on a walk through our new brewery and distillery and finish in the old building. And there you have it: Daens squared.' Flamboyant owners Mike and Roniek set up their brewing-distilling-horeca project at a stone's throw from Sint-Truiden. Amongst an expanse of orchards you discover an authentic industrial site dating back to 1743 which is also home to a new high-tech brewery and distillery, an imposing alcohol distillery from 1890 and a monumental farm with a timbered façade, built in the Haspengouw style, with a café that is perfect for a good chat and a beer tasting. The farm-brewery-distillery dates all the way back to 1642. The buildings in the grounds are imposing in size. The brewery café is located in a timbered barn dating back to 1690. The barn is 42m long and 13m high. **TIP:** visit this brewery when the blossoms are out and walk or ride amongst the fruit trees of idyllic Haspengouw. Sightsee in Sint-Truiden and admire the beguinage.

The playful but informative tour of the alcohol distillery, the brewery and the industrial heritage is only held at 1500 on Saturdays, Sundays and Bank Holidays. Online reservation is required for group visits.

Wilderenlaan 8, Wilderen (Sint-Truiden)
+32(0)11/58 06 80 – info@brouwerijwilderen.be
www.brouwerijwilderen.be

SINT-TRUIDEN

Things to see and do
- the town hall and the belfry
- the ruins of the abbey
- the Minderbroedersite with its church, monastery, gardens and museum
- the beguinage
- the former city walls and the municipal park

Tip: on foot, follow the Monumentenwandeling, signposted with rivets on the pavement, and explore the fruit region of Haspengouw on foot or by bike when the blossoms are out.

Toerisme Sint-Truiden
Grote Markt 36
B-3800 Sint-Truiden
+32(0)11/70 18 18
www.toerisme-sint-truiden.be

↑ Sint-Truiden, tower of the abbey

WORTH A DETOUR

ABDIJ HERKENRODE

Herkenrode

From the exit Hasselt-West on the E313 you can view the impressive silhouette of the former abbey of Herkenrode. Its grounds and buildings date back to the 17th century but this abbey can trace back its history to 1182. Jef Cornelissen Senior of the Cornelissen brewery had the idea of launching an abbey beer. Robert Putman, who used to be engineer-brewmaster with Cristal-Alken, made sure the operation went smoothly. He was tasked with brewing a beer with 'the bravery of the Counts of Loon, the elegance of the Abbesses of Herkenrode and the aromas of the herb garden.' Herkenrode has produced its own recognised abbey beers ever since 2009: Herkenrode Tripel and Bruin. 'Recognised' points to a demonstrable link with the past as there used to be a brewery in the abbey.

Herkenrode is located five kilometres away from Hasselt within a splendid nature reserve (100 ha) ideal for walking and cycling. There is a shop selling regional products and you can relax in the tavern. Guided tours of the herb garden (which contains 250 culinary herbs) are available on request.

Herkenrodeabdij 4, Hasselt
+32(0)11/33 43 70 – www.herkenrode.be
www.abdijsiteherkenrode.be

BOCHOLTER BROUWERIJMUSEUM

The Bocholter Brouwerijmuseum is located across the road from the Martens brewery, known for its pils and Sezoens beer. This museum started collecting in 1919. It tells the story of the art of brewing from 1758 up to the present time. The loft contains everything related to malt and malting. One floor down, in the brewhall, you get lost amongst the filtration basins, boiling kettles and draining basins. The cellars contain bottling equipment as well as imposing wooden barrels used for cold storage of the beer. You will also find a collection of pouring taps, beer pumps, beer pipes and so on. You will find out the workings of steeping basins, malt ploughs, boiling kettles, wort coolers, mashing basins, barrel tarring equipment and many other devices. This museum is highly recommended to beer connoisseurs, hobby brewers and anyone with an interest in traditional brewing techniques. Your visit ends with a tasting of the Martens beer in the tasting room where those with a nostalgic bent will lap up the images on the walls, covered in vintage beer advertising.

Group tours available throughout the year on application. You can visit daily in July and August, from 1300 to 1800, guided tours are held at 1330 and 1530.

Dorpsstraat 53, B-3950 Bocholt
+32(0)89/48 16 76
www.bocholterbrouwerijmuseum.be
of via VVV Bocholt – +32(0)89/20 19 30
toerisme@bocholt.be

BREWING IN BOKRIJK

A municipal decree dating back to 1545 stipulates that the village of Diepenbeek always had to brew at least one 'weak' beer but only one 'dick' or quality beer was required. In het Paenhuys brewing was done using the water from the 'Panisbeek' stream complemented with water from a stone clog fixed to the wall, in other words, an 'opgemetste stenen klompe'. Het Paenhuys is an authentic 17th century village brewery from Diepenbeek. Until 1700 the villagers were able to brew their own beer at Het Paenhuys. The brewery has now been transported to the Bokrijk open air museum. How did people go about brewing in those days? First of all, water was pumped into the heated brewing kettle that was built into the wall. Using buckets, the heated water was then poured into the stirring or mashing basin. Once it had arrived in the basin the crushed malt was stirred using a mashing stick.

Hot water had to be added from time to time to keep the mix at the right temperature. The wort was subsequently filtered, historically using sieving spoons, in later years with the so-called 'stuikmand' that filtered out the rough elements, known as bran or 'bostel'. The remaining liquid was put to the boil once again and at this point, hops were added. This liquid, now going under the name of wort, was then transferred into a large wooden cooling basin, otherwise known as a koelschip, to cool down and re-ferment. It would mature and become saturated by a second fermentation. Yeast cells and other particles were filtered out using linen bags and the beer finished its journey in barrels. The fixtures and fittings of Het Paenhuys have been transported from the former Hoegaarden-based Tomsin brewery. Hoegaarden brewer Pierre Celis learnt his trade at Tomsin before founding De Kluis in 1966. Erf Abele, the Abele farmyard which forms part of the open air museum, now proudly cultivates its own hop field. The museum also displays a traditional hop drying kiln from the village of Proven near Poperinge. An unmissable event is the Day of the Edible Landscape ('De Dag van het Eetbare Landschap'). Every third Sunday in September 1500 litres of craft beer flow from the tanks at Het Paenhuys. A unique reminder of an artisan brewing process steeped in history.

Bokrijk open air museum is open from 31 March – 30 September, every Tuesday – Sunday between 1000 and 1800. Tip: cycle 'through the water' at cycle node point 91, explore the cafés and restaurants in the region and pay a visit to C-Mine in Winterslag (Genk).

Bokrijklaan 1, 3600 Genk – +32(0)11/26 53 00
infobokrijk@limburg.be – www.bokrijk.be

TOERISME LIMBURG
Universiteitslaan 3
B-3500 Hasselt
+32(0)11/30 55 00
info@toerismelimburg.be
www.toerismelimburg.be

↑ Bokrijk, Paenhuys

EUPEN
HUY
LIÈGE
MALMEDY
SPA
STAVELOT
VERVIERS

BELLEVAUX (Brasserie de)

Bellevaux Black, Blanche, Blonde & Brune

What prompted a Dutchman to start brewing on the edge of the Hoge Venen area? 'I gained my pharmacy degree in Utrecht and, in this student city, I became familiar with a wide range of beers,' Wil Schuwer, the brewer, tell us, whilst enjoying a glass of fruity white beer. 'It grew into a passion. I often visited breweries and, deep within me, the plan fermented to start brewing myself some time in the future. We started brewing in 2006.' Bellevaux now produces a 'blanche' white beer, a 'brune' with a high malt content, a 'blonde' and a 'black' that is a lot like stout. 'Part of the taste is determined by the sourish water from the fens,' the brewer explains. 'Just try this one!' he urges whilst pouring me a glass of raspberry beer. His son Tom has now taken over the mashing stick: 'Half of the white beer we produce is used for steeping raspberries. This is our raspberry beer. We use three varieties of dry hops, several types of malt and spices like coriander and dried orange peel. Elderflower is added to the white beer.' The jet-black stout Bellevaux Black avoids drying out the taste buds thanks to the successful balance between sweet, roast and bitter with touches of butter caramel. A hop field is being established uphill from the brewery. This is where the brewers experiment with different varieties.

TIP: there are five 'beer walks' (1.5km – 14.5km) that start from the brewery.

The tasting room is open every weekend except January from 1100 to 1800. Guided tours are held every Saturday and Sunday at 1600. Group visits (10 or more guests) are available on request.

Bellevaux 5, Malmedy
+32(0)80/88 15 40
brasserie@brasseriedebellevaux.be
www.brasseriedebellevaux.be

MALMEDY

Things to see and do
- the Cathedral and the carillion
- the Malmundarium museum about the history of the city, in the grounds of the former abbey
- the Baugnez 44 Historical Center about the Second World War
- the valley of the Warche and Reinhardstein Castle

Tip: visit the city during its annual carnival

Tourisme Malmedy
Rue Jules Steinbach 1
B-4960 Malmedy
+32(0)80/79 96 66
www.malmedy.be

BOTTERESSE (La)

La Botteresse, Sur-les-Bois, seizoensbieren

We meet in a converted garage. In 1996 José Poncin, a chemical scientist, started brewing here. Scientific precision is second nature to him. The name of 'La Botteresse' is reminiscent of the women who used to carry the hops. The brewer was in search of his own personal signature and found it through the use of herbs such as juniper berries – known for its use in Dutch gin or *peket* – and sage. José is keen on rich, full-mouthed beers with a rich hop content. To this end he is experimenting with American hop varieties like Amarillo and Citra. His honey beer has a surprisingly zesty character. It turns out this is no coincidence. 'It contains as many as twelve different varieties of herbs,' José reveals. **TIP:** visit the Castles of Jehay and Warfusée, the Maîtres du Feu experience centre or the Amay bicycle museum.

Visit by prior arrangement for groups of 10 and over.

Rue Fond Méan 6, Saint-Georges
+32(0)477/17 79 27 – info@labotteresse.be
www.labotteresse.be

BRASSE & VOUS

Esperluette, Legia

Bruno Bonacchelli is a brewer steeped in experience. He installs industrial brewing filters and as such is familiar with large breweries. However, at his own microbrewery on the edge of Liège, he is happy to steer his own course. Under the name of 'Legia' Bruno produces a range of predominantly light beers that pack in a surprising amount of flavour. He does not tend to use herbs and spices except for the feather-light and refreshing Legia Cassis & Menthe (mint). However, Bruno doesn't mind the odd experiment. How about a beer brewed with shoots of the Douglas Fir or else one with smoky aromas? Bruno has pledged himself to his Legia Blonde. Esperluette is the name of a range of degustation beers that includes an amber beer. Ask the brewer if there is 'anything special' on offer – seasonal beers are on offer from time to time. Enjoy the beers and the regional cuisine at Le Réfectoire de la Brasserie, the restaurant located in the brewhall. With any luck, you will see the brewer at work.. **TIP:** sightseeing in Liège .

Open on Thursday, Friday and Saturday night. Get in touch with the brewery to arrange your visit.

Rue d'Alleur 27c, Liège
+32(0)4/384 84 78
www.brasse-et-vous.be

LIÈGE

Things to see and do
- the Place Saint-Lambert and the Archeoforum
- the former Palais des Princes-Evêques
- the Perron fountain and the city hall
- the Montagne de Bueren staircase and the 'coteaux'
- Maison Curtius and its associated musea
- the Musee de la Boverie for contemporary art
- the Musée de la Vie Wallonne
- the Church of Saint-Barthélémy and its eponymous baptismal font, a feat of medieaval ironwork
- the Outremeuse neighbourhood, the childhood home of writer Georges Simenon
- the Tchantchès museum with its puppet theatre
- the railway station designed by Santiago de Calatrava
- the La Batte Sunday market on the banks of the river Meuse
- the Saint Pholien flea market on Fridays
- the botanic gardens and the arboretum attached to the university
- the aquarium

Tourisme Liège
Place du Marché 2
B-4000 Liège
+32(0)4/221 92 21
www.liège.be
www.luik.be

CURTIUS (Brasserie C)

Black, Curtius, Torpah

Renaud Pirotte and François Dethier met as students. Both read food science in Liège and set up a microbrewery in partnership. They tried out dozens of recipes until the Curtius was born: a light blond beer based on barley and wheat malt, subtly bitter, fruity and aromatic. Unfiltered, unpasteurised, bottle re-fermented and poured into a stylish champagne bottle. 'Our beer's name is symbolic', Renaud explains. 'Curtius was an entrepreneur avant-la-lettre from Liège, who climbed the social ladder to end up a respected aristocrat. His mansion lies on the banks of the river Meuse. This Renaissance palace is now a municipal museum.' Renaud grew up in the shadow of Brasserie d'Achouffe. These gentlemen brewers produce not only Curtius, but also Torpah: an IPA (India Pale Ale) that comes in three different degrees of bitterness. Order a tasting board and compare for yourself. **TIP:** enjoy the bar and the romantic terrace at this unique building – before, during or after your visit to Liège's historic city centre.

Brewery tours by prior arrangement.

Impasse des Ursulines, Liege
+32(0)4/266 06 92 or +32(0)473/59 56 55
info@brasseriec.com
www.brasseriec.com

ELFIQUE

La Redoutable, La Robuste

André Grolet set up this microbrewery in the heart of the Ardennes in the vicinity of the La Heid des Gattes nature reserve and the only real 'mountain river' in our country, the Ninglingspo. He first experienced brewing in Quebec. André used to be a butcher-caterer as well as a farmer in a former life. He has 'pioneer' written all over him. He cobbled together his own brewing equipment. In the near

↑ Amblève   ↓ Stavelot, abbey

future the brewery will move into a fomer glass factory on the site of an old quarry. Have the elves had a hand in making the beer? Make your own judgment. André is taking all the time in the world. He uses fresh yeast for every batch and allows all of his beers to re-ferment. The brewer loves pure tastes and his dry, bitter blonde is proof of this. The amber beer has surprising impressions of caramel and nuts, hazel nuts and cashew nuts for example. The drak triple contains four different malts and two varieties of hops. You can smell quince, plum and sirop de Liège. **TIP:** visit the caves of Remouchamps, the Domaine de Palogne with the ruins of the fortified castle of Logne and Monde Sauvage safari park.
Visit by prior arrangement.

Sur La Heid 23, Aywaille
+32(0)4/263 07 17 – +32(0)473/59 56 55
info@elfique.be
www.elfique.be

> **EUPEN**
>
> **Things to see and do**
> - the city hall and market square
> - mansions, churches and fountains
> - the Wool Route (route de la Laine)
> - Kunst und Bühne, a former sheep shearers' workshop converted into an arts centre
> - the Weser Talsperre experience centre
> - the Vesder barrage and the artificial lake it created
> - the nature reserve of Hoge Venen, the 'roof of Belgium'
>
> **Tip:** visit this city at Rosenmontag, when the carnival is on, or at the time of the Christmas market
>
> **Toerisme Eupen**
> Marktplatz 7
> B-4700 Eupen
> +32(0)87/55 34 50
> info@eupen-info.be
> www.eupen.be

EUPENER BRAUEREI

Cabane

Civil servant Norbert Heukemes set up his pico or nano brewery in his garage in its idyllic location at an old water mill and a river in the Hoge Venen (Hautes Fagnes) region, which accounts for the soft, slightly sour water he uses for brewing. This beer lover and beer traveller is proud to own the 'only brewery in Eupen'. Pale malt, wheat flakes, coriander and curaçao orange peel contribute to the taste of the Cabane Blonde. There is a dark version 'in the pipeline'.

Hütte 48, Eupen
+32(0)479/34 19 39
info@cabane-eupen.be

Eupen

SPA

Things to see and do
- the new Thermes de Spa for a touch of wellness
- the Musée de la Ville des Eaux
- the casino
- the Pouhon Pierre le Grand and other historic wells

Tip: explore the fens and its forests on foot or by mountain bike or on cross-country skis in winter.

Tourisme Spa
Rue du Marché 1A
B-4900 Spa
+32(0)87/79 53 53
info@spatourisme.be
www.spatourisme.be

FLO (Brasserie Artisanale du)

Flo Blanche, Blonde, Ambrée, Brune, Triple en Fruit

After the merger with Hannuit the town hall of Blehen had no further role to play. What was it going to be? A storage space, exhibition rooms or a meeting hall? The Confrérie de Saint Antoine had different ideas: they would install a craft brewery. Why? To promote the tradition of regional beers, go back to the roots and invigorate the village. You can now discover the art of brewing all the way from grinding the malt down to bottling the beer. 'Flo' is named after a hamlet on the banks of the eponymous river that used to run high and low. In the winter months, the river served as a natural ice skating rink. This Haspengouw village also was a regular pilgrimage destination between 1700 and 1935 in honour of Saint-Antoine, patron saint of cattle. The local *confrérie* still bears witness to this tradition.

Visit by prior arrangement.

Rue du Château 2, Blehen (Hannuit)
+32(0)19/51 70 57 of +32(0)495/59 57 59
www.brasserieduflo.be

GRAIN D'ORGE (Brasserie de)

Aubel, Brice, Canaille, Grelotte, Joup, Hervoise

The Land of Herve is an undulating mosaic of meadows bordered by hedgerows and clumps of trees. The farms' grain silos are beacons within a sea of green. This is where Benoît Johnen brews his regional Grain d'Orge beers within the family-owned farm. He proudly shows off his brewing machinery from which the blond Brice, the brown Joup and Schténg flow out of the tanks. Brice and Joup are named after two clans that used to tear the village of Hombourg apart. Beer has tempered the anger. Benoît is a creative brewer who likes to use local produce wherever possible. You can taste the

Land of Herve in the glass, especially in the Hervoise that is based on syrup from apples and pears: fruity, zesty and slightly sour. **TIP:** taste the beer in the Pub Grain d'Orge just around the corner.

Visit by prior arrangement for groups of between 10 and 50.

Rue Laschet 3, Hombourg (Plombières)
+32(0)87/78 77 84
brasserie@grain-dorge.com
www.grain-dorge.com

JUPILLE (Brasserie de)

Jupiler

Belgium's best-selling pils beer is owned by AB Inbev. It all started with a firm that supplied kettles to breweries and decided to produce their own brews in 1853. The brewery was founded by the Piedboeuf family, known at the time for their table beer, and is now one of the largest breweries in the country. Jupiler pils was created in the 1960s when it bore the name of Extra Pils. Jupiler 5 came onto the market in 1966. This beer has conquered Belgian football and the entire country to boot with the slogan 'Men know why.' This should come as no surprise as this brand has been telling the same story ever since 1966. And with a great deal of success – one in two pils beers tapped or poured in Belgium is a Jupiler. The Jupiler name turned into a synonym for pils. Jupille on the outskirts of Liège is now home to one of the largest breweries in the country. The brewhall produces a brew every two hours but the entire production process takes three weeks and involves continuous quality control and tasting. In the brewer's opinion, 'Jupiler has brought pils to a higher standard'. 'All the way from the start, they paid attention to every aspect of quality: from the raw ingredients and how the water was treated down to how the beer was served in cafés and restaurants. Café owners had to have their taps and pipes maintained by Jupiler engineers. This was an obligation rather than a luxury as pils is a very delicate product. If any mistake is made during the brewing or serving process – the beer is too old or the pipes are blocked up - you can taste and smell it immediately. We are able to track everything. When we check the quality of a batch of beer, we know when it was brewed and we can map the entire process.'

This brewery welcomes groups of around 30, Mondays only, between 09.00 and 16.00. Booking essential.

Rue des Anciennes Houblonnières 2,
4020 Jupille-sur-Meuse – +32(0)16/27 61 11
www.breweryvisits.com

↑ Spa

↓ Stavelot, Perron

LIENNE (Brasserie de la)

Grandgousier, Lienne

In 2013 siblings Mélissa and Nicolas Résimont started up this microbrewery in a traditional Ardennes farmhouse. This brewing pair goes for honest beers with a strong sense of 'terroir'. As you find so often in the Ardennes, mystery hangs in the air. Just ask Mélissa to tell you the story of the fairy of the Lienne and the golden goat. Or just check it out on the website. The main fermentation of the Lienne beers is done with yeast from Orval. In the Lienne Blonde, *Dry hopping* provides additional hop aromas whereas the Lienne Brune has touches of caramel and chocolate coming from the roast malt. Lienne Noire is a jet-black *dry stout*. Grandgousier is the hoppiest beer within the range. It is named after the pike that Nicolas catches now and again when he is out fly-fishing. **TIP:** visit the cultural centre in the grounds of the former Stavelot abbey, play a round of 'farmer's golf' in Ferme Monville visit the PlopsaCoo theme park. Enjoy the beers in Le Relais des Pêcheurs in Chevron (www.relaisdespecheurs.be).

Arrange your visit in advance.

> Reharmont 7, Lierneux
> +32(0)80/39 99 06
> info@brasseriedelalienne.be
> www.brasseriedelalienne.be

MARSINNE (Brasserie de)

Léopold 7

Léopold is the embodiment of surrealism. This beer, halfway between a pils and a triple, contains seven ingredients: three grains, three hop varieties and, most importantly, the Léopold touch. Its fate is in the hands of Nicolas Declercq and Tanguy van der Eecken. Tanguy is a scion from a brewing family that, so far, has clocked up one and a half centuries of experience. His great-grandfather purchased the Marsinne castle farm and started to grow barley in its fields. The brewery was acquired by Artois in the 1970s and the rest is history. **TIP:** taste the beer in La Capsulerie in Hannuit.

Visits for groups comprising 10 and over are available on request on Mondays, Thursdays, Fridays and Saturdays.

> Rue de la Médaille 17, Couthuin (Heron)
> +32(0)478/88 25 01
> fannydominique@hotmail.com
> www.leopold7.com

STAVELOT

Things to see and do

- the grounds of the former abbey, converted into a centre of arts and culture
- the church of Saint-Sébastien and its treasures
- the historic, 18th century town centre
- the Amblève, the ancient bridges, fountains, laundries and tanneries
- the Musée du Circuit de Spa Francorchamps for car racing enthusiasts
- the Musée historique de la Principauté de Stavelot-Malmedy about the history of the Prince-Bishops and their realm
- the Musée Guillaume Apollinaire telling the story of this famous French poet

Tourisme Stavelot
Place St-Remacle 32
B-4970 Stavelot
+32(0)80/86 27 06
www.tourisme.stavelot.be

SAINTE NITOUCHE
(Brasserie de la Croix)

Sainte Nitouche

Vincent Lacroix had so many friends urging him to set up a brewery that he finally gave in. At first he started brewing in his own garage but he has now moved into a building better suited to the purpose on an industrial estate on the edge of Liège. First of all he brewed a hefty triple, followed by a white beer using *dry hopping*. 'Whenever an idea comes to me, I put it into practice,' Vincent laughs. 'Sainte-Nitouche' is a nickname for a flirty woman who likes to wind up the men but, at the same time, keeps them at a safe distance. Luckily, this does not apply to the the beer.

Love of the local terroir lives on in the blonde beers, enriched with apple juice from the fruit region of Herve, birthplace of the sirop de Liège. Find out which seasonal beers are available. **TIP:** visit Liège.

Sainte-Nitouche is open every Saturday. You can buy the beer here as well. The brewery opens on request on other days.

Rue des Cerisiers 48, Beyne Heusay
+32(0)476/37 20 06 – info@saintenitouche.be
www.saintenitouche.be

VAL-DIEU (Abbaye de)

Val-Dieu

There is an active brewery in the grounds of the former abbey of Val-Dieu. The former Cistercian abbey was founded 1216 and survived the French Revolution. The current buildings date from the 17th and 18th century. Val-Dieu is a monument to Maasland renaissance interspersed with Romanesque and Gothic influences. The abbey church was re-built in the 19th century. The last monk left in 2001. The central courtyard has agriculture written all over it: the stables, the barn and the mill. The brewery building was torn down at the

---

HUY

Things to see and do
- the citadel
- the church of Notre-Dame de Huyk with its leaded glass windows
- the Grote Markt (main market square) and
- the town hall
- the Pont de Fer
- the ancient neighbourhood surrounding the Hospice Saint Jacques
- the Musée de Huy in the former Capucin abbey
- Jehay Castle and the collections assembled by Guy Van den Steen, Lord of the Manor

Tourisme Huy
1 Quai de Namur
B-4500 Huy
+32(0)85/21 29 15
tourisme@huy.be
www.huy.be
close insert

beginning of the 19th century but since 1997 the smell of malt once again wafts around the courtyard. Beer is now brewed in the former abbey farm, based on the monks' traditional recipes. Val-Dieu stands for unpasteurised, top-fermented beer without the addition of aromatic agents. Its Grand Cru contains pils malt and roast malt. You can taste wine, caramel and speculaas (a spiced shortcrust biscuit); the finish is dry with a pinch of roast malt. A beer you could lay down in your cellar to see what happens. Tip: Val-Dieu makes a great starting point for a tour of the slightly hilly Land of Herve, known for its fragrant cheeses and its syrup.

Group tours of the abbey and brewery on request for 15 – 70 guests.

> Val-Dieu 225, Aubel
> +32(0)87/69 28 28
> infotourist@val-dieu.net
> www.val-dieu.com

WARSAGE

Bière de Warsage

Dominique Denis, an agricultural engineer, aims to brew natural, unfiltered beers that re-ferment in the bottle. His signature beers are fruity with aromas of citrus (blond), apple and pear (tripel) and caramel and banana (brown). Tip: visit the former coal mine at Blegny, the Fort of Eben-Emael and the Tower of Eben-Ezer. Taste the beers at the BeerLoversCafé (www.beer-lovers.be) right in the centre of Liège.

Visits by request.

> Rue Muller 93, Bombaye
> +32(0)474/06 04 34
> info@brasseriewarsage.be
> www.brasseriewarsage.be

VERVIERS

Things to see and do
- the town hall and the market square
- the Maison de l'Eau, an experience centre focused on water
- the Centre Touristique de La Laine et de la Mode about the wool trade
- the Musée d'Archéologie et Folklore
- the Musée des Beaux-Arts et de la Céramique
- the Parcours des Fontaines
- the Parc de Séroule
- the valley of the Vesdre
- the chocolatiers

Tip: enjoy a relaxing a spa day in Chaudfontaine.

Tourisme Verviers
Rue Jules Cerexhe 86
B-4800 Verviers
+32(0)87/30 79 26
info@paysdevesdre.be
www.paysdevesdre.be/verviers

THINGS TO SEE AND DO

ANTHISNES (BEER MUSEUM)

During the Middle Ages Anthisnes became an ecclesiastical domain. Representatives of the Church took over the castle. The main building, in the Maasland Renaissance style, dates back to the 17th century. It is a massive square compound with five floors and walls that are up to two metres thick. The two northern towers were destroyed in a fire in 1897. The 12th century donjon is the building that fires up the imagination most of all. It is now home to a beer museum with a lovely collection of bottles and glasses. The visit comprises a guided tour of the castle and the museum. So what is the link between the castle and beer? Ancient documents refer to two village breweries from the year 1000 onwards. You taste the beers of the region in the beautifully vaulted cellars. Regional beers and local produce can be purchased from the museum shop. From time to time you can attend beer workshops in the museum and brewing will be done here in the not too distant future.

Musée de la Bière et du Péket,
Avouerie d'Anthisnes,
avenue de l'Abbaye 19, Anthisnes
+32(0)4/383 63 90
info@avouerie.be
www.avouerie.be

SANKT VITH (BEER MUSEUM)

In a chalet right at the top of Tomberg piste in Sankt Vith, 4500 bottles are awaiting visitors. These bottles are on display and are meant to be admired rather than consumed. The museum has a collection of historic beer bottles, contributed by tourists throughout the years. Tip: pop in during or after a cross-country skiing trip or a hike on foot in or around the Hoge Venen nature reserve.

Skihütte Verkehrsverein 'Wald und Tal' Rodt,
Tomberg, Rodt 77, Sankt Vith
+32(0)80/22 63 01 – info@biermuseum.be
www.biermuseum.be

Montagne de Bueren, Liège

TOURISME PROVINCE DE LIÈGE

1 Place de la République Française
B-4000 Liège
+32 (0)4 237 95 26
www.Liège tourisme.be

DINANT
NAMUR
ROCHEFORT

BERTINCHAMPS (Ferme de)

Bertinchamps

In 2011 brewer Benoît Humblet came across a dilapidated square farmhouse, lost amongst the fields, in Bertinchamps not far from Gembloux. This was an opportunity for the brewer to turn his dreams into reality. Straight away, Benoît involved his entire family in his life's work. After purchasing the farmhouse the family focused on the first renovation. They based themselves at Bertinchamps. 2013 saw the installation of a modern brewhall in a fully renovated barn. In other words: state-of-the-art technology found a home in a historic farmhouse with a history going back more than 700 years. The brewery is gradually taking shape without affecting the traditional character of the square farm. At Bertinchamps the seeds are sown for a new generation of farm beers. **TIP**: discover the splendid lowland château of the nearby village of Corroy-le-Château: a massive silhouette flanked by robust, round towers.

Visit by prior arrangement. On Thursdays, Fridays and Saturdays, Stefan Jacob displays his culinary talents, paired with the Bertinchamps beers.

Ferme de Bertinchamps 4,
Grand-Manil (Gembloux)
+32(0)484/31 85 58
info@bertinchamps.be
www.bertinchamps.be

BROGNE (Abbaye Saint-Gérard de)

Abbaye de Brogne Blonde & Brune

This microbrewery is housed in the pilgrims' hall attached to this former abbey and is now brewing organic abbey beers. **TIP:** Brogne is located in a region where abbeys proliferate. Maredret, Maredsous and Floreffe are not far away.

Visit by prior arrangement.

Place de Brogne 3, Saint-Gérard (Mettet)
info@abbayedebrogne.com
www.abbayedebrogne.be

CARACOLE (Brasserie)

Caracole, Les Bains d'Epices, Nostradamus, Saxo, Tournée Beaurinoise, Triek, Troublette

At Caracole's, things move slowly and fast at the same time. Its brewer, François Tonglet, used to sell regional products from his Namur-based shop but then discovered regional beers and set up his own microbrewery. So where does the snail in the logo come from? 'Ach, we like to pay homage to our city of Namur', François Tonglet says with a laugh. 'Everything here is done slowly and that includes tasting and drinking.' The City of Dinant is close by. Saxo beer pays homage to local hero Adolphe Sax, who invented the saxophone. The brewer emphasises the importance of using the typical yeast to obtain the right taste, in addition to the malt and hop varieties used. 'Our Nostradamus contains five different malt varieties!' So why does he use wood to fire his kettles? 'Wood is our source of energy, always available and affordable', François replies. 'Wood is sustainable. And it smells lovely!'
TIP: visit Dinant, explore the picturesque Meuse Valley or descend the River Lesse in a kajak.

Admission free Wednesdays, Saturdays and Sundays between 1400 and 1900 during the summer months and on Saturdays from 1400-1900 throughout the year, excluding January. Group tours by prior arrangement.

Côte Marie-Thérèse 86, Falmignoul (Dinant)
+32(0)82/74 40 80 of +32(0)475/96 75 32 (gids)
brasserie.caracole@skynet.be

DU BOCQ (Brasserie)

Blanche de Namur, Corsendonck, Deugniet, Fruit Bocq, Gauloise, Saint Benoît, Saison 1858, Triple Moine

Brasserie du Bocq was founded by Martin Belot in 1858. The sixth generation is now in charge. Brasserie du Bocq started off with a table beer but

DINANT

Things to see and do
- the Citadel and the Army Museum
- the Church of Notre Dame
- the Cave of La Merveilleuse
- the Maison de la Pataphonie for an alternative music experience
- the ruins of the forts of Bouvignes, Montaigle and Poilvache
- the small medieval town of Bouvignes and its Maison du Patrimoine Médiéval Mosan
- the Castles of Crupet, Freyr and Vêves Annevoie Gardens

Tip: take a boat trip along the River Meuse towards Givet or navigate the River Lesse by canoe or kayak.

Tourisme Dinant
Avenue Cadoux 8
B-5500 Dinant
+32(0)82/22 28 70
www.dinant-tourisme.be

gradually moved towards the production of stronger beers that evolve in the bottle. Amongst these, Gauloise is the best known beer. It is named after the Gallic fortifications unearthed in the region. Blanche de Namur, a white beer, flows freely at the time of the annual Fêtes de Namur. Du Bocq beers are characterised by the use of herbs and spices – ginger, coriander, aniseed, mint and vanilla – as well as high-quality hops. Brasserie Du Bocq is owned by Kempen-based brewery Corsendonck, known for their eponymous beers. Tip: visit Namur, the citadel and the Valley of the Meuse.

Consult the brewery website to find out which guided tours are available. Group visits must be booked in advance.

Rue de la Brasserie 4, Purnode
+32(0)82/61 07 90 – visite@bocq.be
www.bocq.be

FAGNES (Brasserie des)

Super des Fagnes Blonde, Brune, Griottes, Scotch & Noël, Fagnes au Miel Biologique, Blanche, Cuvée Guillaume, Cuvée Junior, Cuvée Vigneronne, Fruits des Bois, Saison & Quatre Céréales

At Brasserie des Fagnes you can witness the entire brewing process over a meal or incorporated into a beer tasting. This brewery is home to a museum that focuses on the brewing trade between 1858 and 1970. Beer festivals are staged annually in the second weekend of July. 'Just take a look at the equipment we retrieved from the Degaucquier brewery from Chimay', the owner, Frédéric Adant, kicks off his story. You can wander around a small, interactive display of vintage lorries, barrel fillers, basins and a wide array of brewing tools. Brasserie des Fagnes is a café brewery. Right in front of his visitors, the brewer shows off his craft from Wednesday to Sunday. Frédéric Adant is a scion from a brewing family. 'My great-grandfather, Constant *le boucher*, nicknamed 'the Butcher', was a champion of Greco-Roman wrestling around the turn of the 20th century. He travelled the world and was a local celebrity. Later on, he set himself up as a beer trader

which gave him the impetus to purchase a small brewery. Before long, the reputation of his beers was spreading: they were said to provide strength and courage. My grandfather took over the business and began selling home-made ice cream in the cafés. In the glory days of Stella Artois he was bottling pils that was transported all the way to south Charleroi. The Degaucquier brewery closed its doors in the 1970s. Luc Piron, the resident brewer, likes to carry out the occasional experiment: he produces small brews to which he adds heather flowers, dandelion, nettles, peach or apricot. Luc is in tune with the seasons, producing a fruit beer in the spring, a thirstquencher for the summer, an amber beer in autumn and a Scotch or Christmas beer for winter. His alcohol-free Junior Beer provides a great alternative to fizzy drinks. 'We brew around fifty different beers per year', Luc Piron tells us. Tip: take a ride on the steam train between Mariembourg and Treignes or else explore the forests of the Viroinval on foot or by bike.

Brasserie des Fagnes is closed on Mondays but is open every day during the holiday months of July and August and also on public holidays if they fall on a Monday. Group visits are welcome by prior arrangement. Just get in touch with the brewery.

Route de Nismes 26, Mariembourg (Couvin)
+32(0)60/31 39 19 of +32(0)60/31 15 70
info@fagnes.be
www.brasseriedesfagnes.com

NAMUR

Things to see and do
- the historic city centre and the banks of the Sambre
- Place Saint-Aubain and the Cathedral
- the Groesbeeck-de Croixmuseum with its 18th century collection of decorative arts
- Le Musée diocésain et trésor de la cathédrale Saint-Aubain (the Museum of Religious Arts with its medieval collection)
- the Félicien Rops Museum showcasing the works of this legendary painter, drawing artist and illustrator
- the Church of Saint-Loup, built in a flamboyant baroque style
- the Marché aux Légumes and its bustling cafés and restaurants
- the imposing Citadel and the Citadel park, affording splendid views of the Valley of the Meuse and the city itself

Tip 1: join a boat trip along the Meuse and visit the nearby city of Dinant; the least unspoilt parts of the Valley of the Meuse are between Dinant and Givet.

Tip 2: visit the annual beer festival held in early July: www.namurcapitaledelabiere.be.

Tourisme Namur
Place de la Station
B-5000 Namur
+32(0)81/24 64 49
info@namurtourisme.be
www.namurtourisme.be

HOUPPE

La Houppe

This story begins with five friends with a great passion for beer and for their home city of Namur. The quintet set up a microbrewery at the former Balon-Perrin brewery. Houppe sounds suspiciously like 'hop'. The gentlemen brewers are aiming high as is evident from their logo. Stilt walkers are engaged in a ferocious battle. This beer is sure to appeal to the échasseurs (stilt walkers) engrained in Namur folklore.

Phone ahead to arrange your visit.

> Avenue de la Plante 49, Namur
> +32(0)475/38 16 64 – info@echasse.be
> www.houppe.be

ROCHEFORT

Things to see and do
- the Grotte de Lorette (Lorette cave)
- the ruins of the Castle of the Counts of Rochefort
- the Archéoparc de Malagne about the Gallo-Roman era
- the Château de Lavaux-Sainte-Anne and the hunt museum
- the Grottes de Han-sur-Lesse
- the Centre du Rail et de la Pierre for railway enthusiasts

Tourisme Rochefort
Rue de Behogne 5
B-5580 Rochefort
+32(0)84/34 51 72
www.rochefort.be
www.valdelesse.be

LESSE (Brasserie de la)

Cambrée, Chinette, Hiveresse, Marie Blanche, Rouge-Croix

In 2010 a group of friends bearing the name of Confrérie Du Busson acquired the equipment of the former La Rochefortoise brewery. After six months of pioneering work the brewery was back in operation. 'We want to establish a network of small local producers. We try to use locally grown organic ingredients whenever we can', the brewer assures us. 'Thanks to the members of our co-operative we managed to sell our beers from the test phase onwards. They were really looking forward to getting their crates. Our members are now our best ambassadors and take pride in their beer.' The brewers choose to use locally grown barley wherever possible and like to experiment with different aromas and herbs and spices. **TIP:** admire the ruins of Rochefort Castle, the Grotte de Lorette or the Domaine des Grottes de Han-sur-Lesse.

Tours held at the weekend by prior arrangement for groups of 10-25.

> Rue du Treux 43B, Eprave (Rochefort)
> +32(0)84/45 75 25 of +32(0)471/51 06 34
> info@brasseriedelalesse.be
> www.brasseriedelalesse.be

Rochefort

ROCHEFORT (Abbaye de Saint-Remy)

Rochefort

Rochefort Abbey, Notre-Dame de Saint-Rémy, is the source of this delicious Trappist beer. A patchwork of woodlands, fields and meadows unveils itself on the way to the Abbey. The buildings are in a somewhat hidden location amidst a green oasis on the edge of this little tourist town. Saint-Rémy was first mentioned in the archives in 1230. The current brewery dates back to 1899. The splendid brewhall with its copper boiling and filtration kettles was installed in 1960. 'We use the water from the Tridène spring one kilometre away from the Abbey', Quality Manager Santos Gumer tells us. 'This water is hard which helps the fermentation. Our production schedule is fixed. We brew four times a week and start work at half past three in the morning; by then, the monks have been up for a quarter of an hour. The entire brewing process takes about a week. Once bottled the beer is allowed to rest for at least ten days in the warehouse, where it re-ferments in the bottle.'

Rochefort is a rather modest player in the field of Trappist beers. This is a deliberate choice. One of the brothers: 'We are working hard enough. We are not under stress. Don't forget that we are monks. For us, the brewery is a means to meet our needs and to support our charitable works.' A quiet atmosphere is prized above all. The bottling plant operates one day a week only, as its noise interferes with prayer. The rule of St. Benedict, '*ora et labora*' (pray and work), is strictly applied here. An abbey does not set out to make profits. Neither are compromises made when it comes to quality. The brother is preparing for the weekly degustation ritual, which involves a blind tasting of four bottles wrapped in aluminium foil. All of his senses are finely tuned. He compares the head, tastes the aroma and estimates the age of the beer based on its smell. He is not a newcomer, far from it: he has been doing this job for a quarter of a century. 'We are always the first ones to drink our beer', he laughs. The youngest duo is subjected to a detailed analysis. With the two older beers there is some hesitation… There are at least four years between them, the verdict states. One of the bottles is fifteen years old, which comes as a surprise. The best-before date on the label recommends a storage period of five years. Nevertheless, it turns out that far older beers are still fine to drink. The brother: 'During the first three years, the Rochefort's taste becomes rounder. Afterwards, the beer only evolves very slowly which makes it difficult to pinpoint the date.' Trappist beer is said to be very nourishing. This is far from a coincidence. The monks follow a strict regime that, in earlier days, even prohibited meat, fish and cheese. They needed the nourishing beer to survive. Just like bread, it was an essential foodstuff or, in Dutch, it was 'broodnodig' (as necessary as bread).

The abbey and the brewery are closed to the public.

Rue de l'Abbaye 8, Rochefort
+32(0)84/22 01 47
www.trappistes-rochefort.com

SILENRIEUX (Brasserie de)

Bière d'Autruche, Cuvée des Lacs de l'Eau d'Heure, Joseph, Kriek de Silenrieux, Noël de Silenrieux, Pavé de l'Ours, Sara

In a quiet location in the village of Silenrieux, not far from the well-known Eau d'Heure artificial lake, stands an ancient barn, now converted into a brewery with a bar-restaurant under its roof. Eric Bedoret set up shop here in 1995. Silenrieux supports and promotes the cultivation and use of rare grain varieties and, leading by example, produces beers based on spelt and buckwheat. This 'grain for the poor' thrives on less fertile soil. **TIP:** visit the artificial lakes of L'Eau d'Heure, heaven for water sports aficionados.

Group visits by request. Sample the beers and the local produce at Chez l'Père Sarrasin, the brewery tavern.

Rue Noupré 1, Silenrieux (Cerfontaine)
+32(0)71/63 32 01
brasserie.silenrieux@belgacom.net
www.brasseriedesilenrieux.be

SIGHTSEEING

FLOREFFE (abbey)

Floreffe Abbey was founded in 1121 by Saint Norbert. The abbey church is remarkable for its lovely choir stalls. You are welcome in the church and to visit the abbey gardens. Have a drink and a bite to eat in the millhouse that dates back to the 16th century. Around the year 1250 a brewery and watermill were erected within the abbey walls and the first Floreffe abbey beers were produced soon after. Floreffe Dubbel, Tripel and Prima Melior are now produced by Brasserie Lefèbvre in Quenast.

Rue Séminaire 7, Floreffe
+32(0)81/44 53 03
abbayefloreffe@skynet.be
www.abbaye-de-floreffe.be

LEFFE (museum)

In its idyllic location high above the River Meuse, Hotel La Merveilleuse incorporates La Maison Leffe. The panorama of the city alone, with its Basilica and citadel, is worth a detour. You will not be surprised to hear that this building used to be a... monastery. But don't be mistaken. The Norbertine abbey that has given its name to this beer is located on the opposite bank of the Meuse and on the other side of the city, where the small Leffe river joins the Meuse. The interactive exhibition focuses on the rich history of the abbey and its beer.

Entry is free during the opening hours of the hotel.

La Maison Leffe, Charreau des Capucins 23, Dinant
+32(0)82/22 91 91
www.leffe.com/maisonleffe

LUSTIN (beer museum)

Christian Lejeune, the museum curator, guides you through the dark corridors of his Ali Baba cave. You discover a homage, albeit dusty, to the rich Belgian beer culture. Here, each bottle and each glass comes with its own story or anecdote. No fewer than twenty thousand beer bottles, empty or full, and just as many glasses await the curious gaze of the visitor. All of them are categorised by province and then alphabetically. The ceiling is covered in vintage beer advertising. In a forgotten corner, piles of beer mats are displayed haphazardly. This beer museum is owned by the local beer tasting society Guilde des Tâte-Bières. You can taste and purchase 'just under a thousand' Belgian beers.

Guided tours available on request. Tasting facilities.

Rue de la Gare 19, Lustin
+32(0)81/41 11 02
musee.b.b@skynet.be
www.museebieresbelges.centerall.com

MAREDSOUS (abbey)

Maredsous

Maredsous is the beer served to the Benedictine monks who still live in the eponymous abbey in the Dinant area. The French Revolution heralded the end for many religious institutions. Undeterred, in 1872 Maredsous established a new link with the rich past of this abbey. This is where the monks live, pray and work according to the Rule of St. Benedict (6th century). Maredsous beer is now brewed by Duvel Moortgat. Saint-Joseph, the abbey's visitor centre, is open daily. An excellent venue for tasting traditional abbey specialties such as beer, cheese and bread as well as other, typically Belgian food. Tip: take the rail bike from the former Falaën railway station and glide towards Maredsous using the old railway tracks.

Rue de Maredsous 11, Denée
+32(0)82/69 82 11
www.maredsous.com

TOURISME PROVINCE DE NAMUR
Avenue Reine Astrid 22, B-5000 Namur
+32(0) 81/74 99 00
tourisme@ftpn.be
wwww.ftpn.be

LIST OF BREWERIES PER REGION

Arlon – Bastogne – Bouillon – Durbuy
La Roche – Saint-Hubert

Achouffe (Brasserie d')	12
Bastogne (Brasserie de)	12
Bouillon (Brasserie de)	13
Demanez (Brasserie)	15
Fantôme (Brasserie)	15
GenGoulf (Brasserie)	15
Inter-Pol	17
Lupulus	17
Millevertus (Brasserie artisanale)	17
Orval (Abbaye d')	17
Rulles (La, Brasserie artisanale)	18
Saint-Monon (Brasserie)	19
Sainte-Hélène (Brasserie)	20

Antwerp – Lier – Mechelen – Turnhout

Anker (Het)	24
Antwerpse Brouw Compagnie	25
Brouwershuis ('t)	26
Dochter van de Korenaar (De)	26
Dorpsbrouwerij Humulus	27
Duvel Moortgat	27
Hofbrouwerijke ('t)	28
Hopperd (Den)	28
Koninck (De)	29
Nest (Het)	30
Pakhuis ('t)	30
Pirlot – Kempisch Vuur	31
Scheldebrouwerij	34
Vagebond	34
Weldebrouck	34
Westmalle (Abdij)	36

Ath – Charleroi – Mons – Tournai

Abbaye d'Aulne (Brasserie d')	40
Abbaye de Saint-Ghislain (Brasserie de l')	40
Abbaye des Rocs (Brasserie de l')	41
Art d'en brasser (L')	42
Augrenoise	42
Authentique Brasserie	43
Bièrodrome (Le)	43
Binchoise (La)	43
Blaugies (Brasserie de)	43
Brasserie à Vapeur	45
Brasse-Temps (Le)	46
Brunehaut (Brasserie de)	46
Ça Brasse Pour Moi	47
Carrières (Brasserie des)	47
Caulier (Brasserie)	48
Cazeau (Brasserie de)	52
Chimay (Abbaye de)	52
Deseveaux (Brasserie de)	53
Dubuisson (Brasserie)	53
Dupont (Brasserie)	54
Erquelinnes (Brasserie d')	55
Frasnoise (La)	55
Hoppy (Brasserie)	56
Jean Tout Seul (Brasserie)	56
Légendes (Brasserie des Géants)	57
Légendes (Brasserie Ellezelloise)	57
Pairi Daiza	58
Ranke (De)	58
St-Feuillien (Brasserie)	60
St Lazare (Brasserie de)	61
Scassènes (Brasserie)	61
Silly (Brasserie de)	61
Witches Brewery	62

Bruges – Ieper/Ypres – Kortrijk/Courtrai
Ostend – Poperinge – Roeselare

Alvinne	66
Bie (De)	67
Belgische Originele Moutbakkerij (BOM)	67
Bourgogne des Flandres	68
Bryggja Brewery	68
De Brabandere	71
Dolle Brouwers (De)	72
Eutropius	72
Fort Lapin	73
Gaverhopke ('t)	73
Gulden Spoor (Het)	74
Halve Maan (De)	74

Kazematten	74
Leite (De)	78
Maenhout	78
Omer Vander Ghinste	78
Oude Maalderij (Brouwfirma d')	80
Plukker (De)	84
Rodenbach	85
Seizoensbrouwerij Vandewalle	87
St. Bernardus	87
Siphon Brewing	88
Strubbe	88
Struise Brouwers (De)	89
Toye (Brouwerij)	90
Van Eecke	90
Van Honsebrouck (Castle Brewery)	91
Verhaeghe-Vichte	93
Verzet (Brouwers)	93
Westvleteren (Sint-Sixtusabbey)	94

Brussels – Halle – Leuven/Louvain
Louvain-la-Neuve – Namur – Waterloo – Wavre

AB Inbev (Stella Artois)	98
Affligem Brouwerij	99
Angerik	100
Averbode	100
Beerstorming	100
Belgoobeer	100
Belgo Sapiens Brewers	103
Belle-Vue	103
Block (De)	103
Boon	104
Brabant (La Brasserie du)	105
Brasse-Temps (Le)	105
Brussels Beer Project	106
Cam (De)	106
Cantillon	107
Domus (Huisbrouwerij)	111
3 Fonteinen	111
En Stoemelings	114
Girardin	114
Haacht	115
Hanssens Artisanaal	116
Herberg (Den)	116
Hoegaarden	116

Hof Ten Dormaal	118
Jandrain-Jandrenouille (Brasserie de)	118
Kroon (De)	120
Lefèbvre	120
Lindemans	121
Loterbol	122
Mort Subite	122
Nieuwhuys	124
Oud Beersel	124
Palm Belgian Craft Brewers/De Hoorn	125
Schuur (De)	126
Senne (Brasserie de la)	126
Tilquin (Gueuzerie)	127
Timmermans	127
Triest (Den)	128
Troch (De)	129
Tubize (Brasserie de)	130
Van Campenhout	130
Villers-la-Ville (Abbaye de)	131
Vissenaken	131
Vlier (De)	133
Waterloo (Brasserie de)	133

Aalst – Ghent – Geraardsbergen – Ninove
Oudenaarde – Sint-Niklaas

Boelens	140
Bosteels	140
Cnudde	141
Contreras	142
Danny	142
De Ryck	143
Dilewyns	144
Donum Ignis	144
Glazen Toren (De)	145
Graal (De)	146
Gruut (Stadsbrouwerij)	146
Huyghe	149
Kroontje ('t)	152
Liefmans	152
Malheur (De Landtsheer)	153
Paenhuys ('t)	154
Roman	154
Sint Canarus	156
Slaghmuylder	156

Smisje	157
Tseut (Den)	158
Van den Bossche	158
Van Steenberge	159

Genk – Hasselt – Maaseik – Sint-Truiden Tongeren

Achelse Kluis (De) (Benedictine abbey)	162
Alken-Maes	163
Amai	163
Amburon Belgian Craftbewery	164
Cornelissen (Village Brewery)	164
Engilsen	165
Jessenhofke	167
Kerkom	167
Martens	170
Perron Bieren	170
Ter Dolen (Castle Brewery)	170
Toetëlèr (Den)	172
Wilderen	172

Eupen – Huy – Liège – Malmedy – Spa Stavelot – Verviers

Bellevaux (Brasserie de)	178
Botteresse (La)	179
Brasse & Vous	179
Curtius (Brasserie C)	180
Elfique	180
Eupener Brauerei	182
Flo (Brasserie Artisanale du)	184
Grain d'Orge (Brasserie de)	184
Jupille (Brasserie de)	185
Lienne (Brasserie de la)	187
Marsinne (Brasserie de)	187
Sainte Nitouche (Brasserie de la Croix)	188
Val-Dieu (Abbaye de)	188
Warsage	190

Dinant – Namur – Rochefort

Bertinchamps (Ferme de)	194
Brogne (Abbaye Saint-Gérard de)	194
Caracole (Brasserie)	195
Du Bocq (Brasserie)	195
Fagnes (Brasserie des)	196
Houppe	198
Lesse (Brasserie de la)	198
Rochefort (Abbaye de Saint-Remy)	200
Silenrieux (Brasserie de)	201

Beer museums and brewery museums

Beer Museum Anthisnes	191
Beer Museum Lustin	202
Beer Museum Olen	37
Beer Museum Sankt Vith	191
Beer Museum Schaarbeek	136
Bocholter Brewery Museum	174
De Lambiek Visitors' Centre	124, 134
De Snoek brewery museum	95
Grimbergen abbey beer museum	134
Hop Museum Poperinge	95
Museum of the Belgian brewers, Brussels	136
Paenhuys (Het) Bokrijk	154, 174

Index of towns and cities

Aalst	139
Aarlen	11
Antwerp	23
Ath	39
Bastogne/ Bastenaken	11
Bouillon	11
Bruges	65
Brussels	97
Charleroi	39
Dinant	193
Durbuy	11
Eupen	177
Genk	161
Geraardsbergen	139
Ghent	139
Halle	97
Hasselt	161
Huy/Hoei	177
Ieper/Ypres	65
Kortrijk/Courtrai	65
La Roche	11
Leuven	97
Liège/ Luik	177
Lier	23
Louvain-la-Neuve	97
Maaseik	161
Malmedy	177
Mechelen	23
Mons/Bergen	39
Namur/ Namen	193
Ninove	139
Nivelles/Nijvel	97
Ostend	65
Oudenaarde	139
Poperinge	65
Rochefort	193
Roeselare	65
Saint-Hubert	11
Sint-Niklaas	139
Sint-Truiden	161
Spa	177
Stavelot	177
Tongeren	161
Tournai/ Doornik	39
Turnhout	23
Verviers	177
Waterloo	97
Wavre/Waver	97

Acknowledgements

I would like to thank the following people in particular for their kind and enjoyable co-operation: François-Xavier Allard (Fédération du Tourisme du Hainaut) Floriane De Decker (Fédération du Tourisme du Brabant Wallon) Vital Geeraerts (Toerisme Vlaams-Brabant) Marie-Hélène Gillis (Fédération du Tourisme de la Province de Namur) Ronny Luyckx (Toerisme Limburg) Dirk Marteel (Westtoer) Michael Mathot (Fédération du Tourisme de la Province de Liège) Morgane Vander Linden (Wallonie Bruxelles Tourisme) Frank Vansteeland (Westtoer) Leentje Verlinden (Toerisme Limburg) Pascal Willems (Fédération du Tourisme du Luxembourg Belge)

Once again, many thanks to all!

Erik Verdonck

WWW.LANNOO.COM
Register on our web site and we will regularly send you a newsletter
with information about new books and interesting, exclusive offers.

Text: Erik Verdonck
Photography: Erik Verdonck
English translation: Hoppy Media
Design: Bart Luijten

If you have observations or questions,
please contact our editorial office:
redactielifestyle@lannoo.com

© Lannoo Publishers, Tielt, 2017
D/2017/45/227 – NUR 440
ISBN: 978 94 014 4147 6

All rights reserved. Nothing from this publication may be copied,
stored in an automated database and/or be made public in any form
or in any way, either electronic, mechanical or in any other manner
without the prior written consent of the publisher.